MW00364108

BIBLICAL DOGMATICS

Biblical Dogmatics

By A.G. Voigt

Edited by Jordan Cooper

Just and Sinner Publications

Fairfield, IA 2013

TABLE OF CONTENTS

INTRODUCTION

The practice of Dogmatic theology has been largely neglected in contemporary Lutheranism. There have been no major Dogmatics textbooks like the present one produced in a number of years. The republication of this work is meant to supplement the lack of introductory Dogmatics texts, especially for those who are unable to afford and comprehend Gerhard's *Theological Commonplaces* or Pieper's *Christian Dogmatics*.

Voigt's work is an ideal introduction to the most prominent themes in Lutheran Dogmatics. These chapters are taken from notes that Voigt compiled while teaching Dogmatic theology at the Lutheran Theological Southern Seminary in Columbia, South Carolina. Voigt's experience teaching is evident in this work, as it is readable to one who is not well acquainted with academic theological terminology. Voigt avoids excessive use of Latin and German in the work.

The book is called *Biblical Dogmatics*, as opposed to *Christian Dogmatics*, or *Lutheran Dogmatics*. As the title suggests, Voigt's purpose in this work is to approach Dogmatics from a purely Scriptural point of view. His focus is thus on the exegesis of the text of Scripture, rather than recounting various historical controversies that arose around specific doctrines. This allows him to distinguish between a Dogmatic and Biblical use of various terms and concepts.

Voigt is faithful to the Biblical text. He approaches the text as the Word of God without qualification. He lived in an era where the inspiration of the Bible was often challenged, and theologians rejected the assumption that its words were trustworthy. Voigt avoids getting into any extensive discussion about the transmission or authorship of the Biblical text, but proceeds with the conviction that the current Bible he is working with is nothing other than the pure Word of God.

Along with being Biblically rooted, Voigt is also grounded within the Confessional Lutheran tradition. He discusses theology using the *loci* method which has been standard Lutheran practice since the writing of Philip Melanchthon. In this approach, theology is discussed topic by topic, expounding upon the Biblical testimony to these various subjects in order. Voigt follows many of the standard categories and arguments of the 17th and 18th century scholastic writers, though he at times admits to disagreement on various points.

This work has not been extensively edited due to its clarity of language. Being written in 1916, the language is not thoroughly outdated or unreadable. Throughout the text I have changed certain phrases and words to enhance readability, but the editing is minimal. May this work strengthen your faith and knowledge of Christ.

Jordan Cooper
2013

PREFACE

This book contains the substance of the lectures which for a number of years I have been giving to my classes in Dogmatics. At the request of my friend, the Rev. J. W. Horine, D. D., Manager of the Board of Publication of the United Synod of the Evangelical Lutheran Church in the South, it has been turned over to the Board for publication. The title of the book is also his suggestion. I was inclined to call it simply A Brief Dogmatics. I am aware that the title Biblical Dogmatics is open to just criticism, chiefly because of possible confusion with what is called in theological study Biblical Theology. But the title chosen will serve to indicate my conviction that Christian doctrine is biblical doctrine. In so brief a discussion of the great subject of which the book treats I thought an index was not necessary.

A.G. Voigt. Columbia, S. C, August, 1916

INTRODUCTION

THIS introduction will define dogmatics, describe the essence of Christianity, its foundation in revelation, the source of Christian doctrines, and sketch a scheme by which the principal heads of Christian doctrine may be suitably arranged.

THE SUBJECT DEFINED.

Dogmatics is the systematic presentation of the doctrines of Christianity.
It is customary to divide the study of theology in theology into four departments: exegetical, historical, systematic and practical. Dogmatics is a branch of systematic theology. It applies the results of exegetical study of the Bible and of the historical study of Christianity to the connected and orderly presentation of the truths of the Christian religion. The eminent German theologian, F. H. R. Frank, called his dogmatics "The System of Christian Truth." That is what dogmatics aims to be.

System is not simply arrangement, but such arrangement as shows the interrelation, the connection and dependence of the parts which constitute a whole. For example, the arrangement of doctrinal material, introduced by Melanchthon and in vogue for some time after the Reformation, under heads called Loci, did not constitute a system. The name Dogmatics, first applied in the seventeenth century, came into general use in the eighteenth century, as in Buddeus' *Institutiones Theologiae Dogmaticae*.

The name suggests that dogmatics is the science of the dogmas of the Church. But this is not the fact. A dogma is a fixed, accepted teaching of the Church. But a writer on dogmatics is not a mere historian or defender of the doctrines officially received in the Church. He states his own Christian beliefs. As the word dogmatic is now used in theology, it only means beliefs laid down in definite propositions and systematic order. A German name for this branch of theology, used by Schleiermacher, is *Glaubenslehre*, i. e., the doctrine of the faith. Dogmatics does not fully present every side of Christian truth. One side is presented by Ethics. Dogmatics exhibits the truth of Christianity as coming from God and working from above upon man and the world. Ethics exhibits Christian truth as working in men, producing an attitude of soul towards God and of conduct towards men.

THE ESSENCE OF CHRISTIANITY.

Christianity is religion in its most perfect form. Its distinguishing feature is that in it the relations between God and man are mediated by Christ.

The proposition: "Christianity is religion in the most perfect form," is designed to mark the uniqueness of Christianity, not to class it among the religions of the world. Philosophy tries to deduce the essence of religion from the nature of man and his position in the universe. By its method it can arrive at only the most general features of religion, not at the most perfect religion. The science of religion seeks by historical study and comparison to determine the essential characteristics of religion inductively. But it can only determine certain phases of religious life, not the true religion.

The study of Christian doctrine must view the question of the essence of religion from the standpoint of Christianity, which assumes that true religion is given from above. It begins with the judgment of faith that the Christian has the true religion. From this point of view Christianity is not a religion among others, but religion absolutely. It is the standard by which the elements of truth in the religions of the world are to be appraised. It cannot admit a standard of philosophy or science, by which its character as religion is to be determined.

Religion is life in the consciousness of the relations that exist between God, man and the world. The essential characteristic of Christianity is that all these relations center in Christ. In Him God is perfectly revealed, man is redeemed, and the world is being prepared for perfect order. Jesus Christ is a historical person, but He is in eternal union with God, and the fellowship of man with God and the establishment of God's kingdom in the world are made possible by Him. He is the Redeemer of the world, who overcomes the alienation of men from God caused by sin through His work of atonement. He is the source of the moral renewal of mankind by His Spirit, which He imparts. The unity and harmony of God, man and the world, shall be completed in Christ.

THE FOUNDATION OF CHRISTIANITY IN REVELATION

Christianity is the religion of divine revelation. Its origin and saving power are due to the personal manifestation of God, whereby the relations which ought to subsist between God and man are made known.

It has been said that all religions rest upon revelation. But then the word revelation is used in a vague sense to express the idea that any consciousness of the divine in man is implanted by God. Christianity claims to be the result of a special operation of God. Its origin cannot be compared to that of any other religion. Even the people of the Old Testament had the consciousness of special revelation. "He hath not dealt so with any nation." Ps. 147:20.

REVELATION DEFINED.

Revelation is the action of God by which He makes Himself known with the view of bringing men into His fellowship.

Revelation is here defined as the action of God because it is not a mere imparting of information of what He requires or promises. God manifests Himself in act, in a connected succession of historical acts. But the definition includes that God gives knowledge of Himself. Word accompanies the acts as their necessary interpretation. Revelation is more than divinely directed history, which teaches lessons. Such history would speak only indistinctly to man. God explains His actions by His accompanying word. The word is the enduring part of the revelation.

The end in view is an essential part of revelation. That end is fellowship with God. Not all knowledge of truth, not even all knowledge of God is revelation. Philosophy and science develop truth, but they are not revelation.

> "In the sense of the Bible and of the Church, revelation must be distinguished from the working of God in the world generally, because it belongs to the sphere of personal intercourse with God." (Kaehler)

The Bible contains the revelation of God, and it is the enduring revelation of God. It itself contains no definition of revelation. Even the biblical terms which mean to reveal are used in a general sense. But the Bible everywhere presents God as manifesting Himself to men in wider or more special relations by act and word; and the writers of the books of the Bible exhibit men as speaking the Word of God, or write as themselves declaring God-given truth.

In the history of the Church the idea of revelation underwent no vital changes until a recent period. The early Church laid stress upon the element of knowledge in revelation. It was viewed as a source of doctrines. Religious truth outside of Christianity was regarded also as given by revelation. The scholastics of the Middle Ages distinguished between general or natural revelation and special or supernatural revelation. The Reformation eliminated tradition from revelation and limited it to the Scriptures. Protestant orthodoxy of the seventeenth century stressed the element of knowledge and practically identified revelation with the production of the Bible. This overemphasis upon the element of knowledge led in the eighteenth century to the valuation of revelation as a supplement to reason, and to the discussion of the possibility and necessity of such a supplement. The nineteenth century approached the subject of revelation from the historical and psychological side.

On the one side the element of divine manifestation in deeds was made prominent, at the same time the element of knowledge being retained. On the other side revelation was reduced to that unknown factor which accounts for the origin of religion in the human soul. According to this view the revelation really occurs in the religious human consciousness, but this consciousness may be awakened by God's working in the history of salvation or by the historical Christ. Fundamental differences in modern thought come into view here. We cannot admit that the originality of the consciousness of God, which the Founder of our religion possessed in a higher degree than others, is not specifically different from what others can and must experience. The experience of Christ's followers is not the same in kind as He had in a superlative degree, but it is an effect of what He revealed. Nor is the experience of prophets and apostles our experience, for we become believers through their word.

THE SOURCE OF CHRISTIAN DOCTRINE.

The only ultimate source of Christian doctrine is the revelation of God contained in the Bible. The doctrine of inspiration will not be discussed here.

Inspiration belongs to the work of the Holy Spirit, and it will receive consideration under that head. The inspiration of the Holy Scriptures, as essential to the fact that in the Scriptures we have the revelation of God, is assumed here.

The question at issue at this point is in regard to the ultimate authoritative source of the knowledge of Christian doctrine, or as it has been expressed, the seat of authority in Christian belief. The definition given is positive. Nevertheless it is recognized that the question involved is a complicated one. For when we consider how a Christian comes to accept the beliefs which he holds, we cannot but observe that a number of factors are involved. He has learned them in the Church; he has acquired them by the use of his mind; he has proved them in his experience; he has directly or indirectly been taught from the Bible. It is therefore not surprising that, together with the Bible, the Church and the reason and consciousness of man have been regarded as sources of Christian doctrine.

The question at issue is not what factors enter in as modifying influences in the production of the beliefs and teachings of Christians, but what is the ultimate authoritative source of the knowledge of Christian doctrine. The Roman Catholic Church finds this seat of authority in the Church, which has divine and infallible authority. In the exercise of this authority it has defined the Bible and tradition to be the sources of its teachings.

The Reformation rejected the authority of the Protestant Church as final, and excluded tradition from the sources of divine teaching. It made the Bible the source and norm of Christian truth. In the nineteenth century this was called the formal principle of Protestantism.

Rationalism, whatever value it may place upon the Church and the Bible practically, in the end makes human reason the ultimate arbiter of what is to be believed. It exalts the subjective principle of knowledge to the supreme place. In this respect mysticism is like it, for mysticism exalts the inner light or inward experience above objective sources of doctrine, such as the Church or the Bible.

We stand firmly on the position of the Reformation. From it we form our estimate of the Church and of human reason in relation to Christian doctrine. The Church has undoubtedly much to do with the determination of doctrine as confessed by us. As a divine institution the Church has the function of teaching. The verities of the Christian faith are received by the theologian through the ministration of the Church. But the Church does not make doctrines. It receives them, and it receives them through the Scriptures. The Church is not an authoritative judge of the truth, but a ministering institution to impart the truth which it has itself derived from the Bible.

For the rationalist God really reveals Himself in the consciousness of man. The Scriptures are only a record of how God revealed Himself in the consciousness of men in the past. The Church is only a society holding certain religious tenets. In opposition to such subjectivism it must be maintained that reason and inward experience do not originate Christian truth; they appropriate it. Certainly inward appropriation by thought, feeling and will is necessary for personal realization of the truth. But there can be no Christian experience and knowledge unless the content of it is given in the objective revelation of God, which we have in the Bible.

In recent years much has been said of "the historical Christ" as the revelation of God. This "historical Christ" is not the Christ of the Gospel story, but "the inner life," the soul of Jesus. It is conceived that we learn the truth by an overwhelming impression of this august personality, who in His sublime life exhibited what true religion is. This is really a mystical and rationalistic view, which gives a qualified recognition to the Bible. As far as this theory makes Christianity essentially subjective, it has the weakness of rationalism. As far as it gives recognition to an objective Christ, it is driven to the Scriptures as the source of the knowledge of the truth.

Brief notice must also be taken here of the difficulty created for faith in the Bible by historical criticism. The Scriptures are the record of revelation. Now criticism raises the question, whether we must abide by the record as it is, or must we penetrate through it as a veil to get to the real facts and the essential revelation. It is not the province of dogmatics to prescribe what methods historical criticism shall pursue. But dogmatics must take a stand in reference to the

Bible, upon which criticism operates. Our position is this: whatever criticism may prove to have been the processes by which the Bible came to be what it now is, we must use it as the revelation of God as it is. In our use of the Bible in this book we shall not stop and inquire whether any statement, properly authenticated as a part of the text, ought to be a part of the record.[1]

CONFESSIONAL CHARACTER OF DOGMATICS.

Dogmatics is the statement of Christian truth as it is known and confessed in the Church. Theology is not pure science. It exists for the Church and its high purposes. A writer may present the teaching of Christianity as he conceives it individually; but even in such a case he would not stand outside of the Church. His work would aim at correcting, if necessary, the established teaching of the Church. If a dogmatics does not reflect the confessional teaching of the Church, it aims to show what the confessional teaching should be. Ordinarily a writer stands in professed connection with some part of the Church and represents Christianity as it is known and confessed in it.

But confessionalism does not mean that it is the office of dogmatics simply to reproduce and defend the accepted doctrines of the Church. This was the conception in the seventeenth century. But it is the function of theology to develop further the known doctrines. It looks not only to the

---

[1] Voigt avoids discussing the historical critical issues here, simply being content to affirm the truth of the text as it has been received by the church. Whatever the means by which these books were compiled are irrelevant according to Voigt, so long as the veracity of the completed text is confessed.

past, but also to the present and the future. Moreover, the possibility of needed correction of traditional belief must always be reckoned with. Christians must ever search the Scriptures to obtain fuller, purer and better views of the truth. However, efforts at new development of Christian doctrine ought not to be carried on regardless of the truth that has already been attained and of Church confessions.

ORDER OF TREATMENT.

The arrangement of the material of dogmatics should be logical, flowing from the central idea of Christianity. That central idea is the communion of man with God through Christ. The history of this communion displays the logic of it. Its ground in God must be considered first. Its establishment in the creation of man comes next. Then follows the disturbance of it by sin. Its restoration in the redemption of Christ is the heart of the whole. Its consummation in the world to come forms the conclusion.

Technical terms have long been in use to designate the principal heads of Christian doctrine. Such terms are these: theology, the doctrine of God; anthropology, the doctrine of man; soteriology, the doctrine of salvation; Christology, the doctrine of Christ; pneumatology, the doctrine of the Holy Spirit; ecclesiology, the doctrine of the Church; and eschatology, the doctrine of the future. The scheme of arrangement, which shall be followed in this book, is as follows:

The Communion of Man with God through Jesus Christ:
1. Grounded in God,
2. Established in the Creation of the World and of Man,

3. Disturbed by Sin,

4. Restored in the Redemption through Christ;

      a) Provided in the Gracious Purpose of God,

      b) Realized in the Person and Work of Christ,

      c) Applied by the Holy Spirit in the Church through the Means of Grace ;

5. Consummated in the World to Come.

CHAPTER I
GOD
THE COMMUNION OF MAN WITH GOD GROUNDED IN GOD.

THE SOURCE OF COMMUNION WITH GOD.
The fellowship of man with God must be traced back to the being of God. There is its ground and source. Such fellowship exists because God is personal, and is life, light and love.

The central truth of Christianity is that the true relation between God and man is one of communion, a communion that exists through the mediation of Jesus Christ. "Our fellowship is with the Father, and with His Son Jesus Christ," 1 Jn 1:3. It is not for a mere formal reason that the idea and nature of God are first discussed in the study of Christian doctrine. He is the fountain and foundation of all life, and so of all that pertains to the right relation of man to Him. The establishment of that relation, the power by which it exists, and all the benefits which flow from it, have their basis, not in the world or in man, but in God. This truth presupposes a conception of God which corresponds with the life and salvation, in the giving of which He reveals Himself. As the ground of all fellowship, life and salvation for man, God is Father, Son and Holy Spirit, and He is, as St. John emphasizes, life, light and love. Cf. Jn 5:26; 1 Jn 1:5; 4:8, 16; 5:20.

THE CHRISTIAN CONCEPTION OF GOD.

The Christian doctrine of God is that of the God of revelation, that is, of God as He has revealed Himself and as He is described in the Holy Scriptures.

This proposition is laid down as a protest against the introduction of abstract philosophical ideas about pure and absolute being into theology. The history of theology from early times betrays the influence of metaphysical speculations imported from philosophy. Such influences are perceptible in early Christian theologians, notably, Origen; in the scholastics of the Middle Ages; in some degree also in the orthodox theology of the seventeenth century; and to a large extent in more recent theology. Since the truth of Christianity is fundamentally set forth in the Scriptures, the Christian idea of God should be sought in them. In laying down this method, it is not intended to cast invidious reflections upon philosophy in its place, nor to detract from the value of natural theology. For apologetic purposes the natural knowledge of God must be highly appreciated, and even in the study of Christianity it must be recognized as an evidence of the redeemability of man. But the Christian does not get his idea of God from mere natural knowledge or philosophy. He derives it from the revelation of God described in the Bible. God makes Himself known.

THE KNOWLEDGE OF GOD.

God is known by His self-revelation. To distinguish different spheres of this self-revelation the terms natural and supernatural are employed.

The truth that God is known by revelation needs to be emphasized. The true idea of revelation is an action of God by which He manifests Himself in some side of His being. God is not a mere idea of the human mind, a generalization of human thinking that something lies behind all the phenomena of the world. The mind of man does not evolve the true idea of God out of its processes; it grasps it when God in some way manifests His presence in the life of man. God is known only as He has made Himself known. The human race did not rise gradually to the idea of God by an evolution. There was a revelation of God from the beginning of the human race. What history and anthropology show is not a progression to the true idea of God, but a perversion and corruption of truth originally given.

From the Scriptures we learn how God has made Himself known, namely, through act and word, through operations in nature and operations that transcend the workings of nature. The whole course of revelation, of the action by which God manifests Himself, constitutes a history that culminates in Christ. God is fully made known in Christ. "No man hath seen God at any time; the only begotten Son, who is in the bosom of the Father, He hath declared Him." Jn 1:18.

The Bible contains no proof for the existence of God. The Old Testament simply assumes that Jehovah is the only and true God. The New Testament assumes that the Father of the Lord Jesus Christ is the same only and true God. No proof of the existence of God is necessary in the Bible, because it teaches the universal revelation of God, however this revelation has been corrupted in heathenism. The doctrine of St. Paul is especially explicit on this point.

When the Scriptures speak of revelation, the terms used never imply a contrast between natural and supernatural revelation. They are general. However, there is a valid distinction between natural and supernatural revelation, not as indicating two modes of obtaining knowledge of God, one without, the other with God's action. All revelation is by God's action. The distinction refers to the spheres of God's activity, on the one hand in nature and the conscience of man, on the other in special supernatural acts. The Bible recognizes both.

God can be really known. The incomprehensibility of God denies full knowledge, but not real knowledge. Even the imperfect and confused ideas of heathenism have elements of real knowledge of God in them. The revelation of God is a true manifestation of what He is. The anthropomorphisms of human language in speaking of God, in which the Bible abounds, signify the inadequacy of human expression, but not the unreality of God's nature symbolized in them. They denote the personal relations and characteristics of God.

THE NATURAL REVELATION OF GOD.

This is the revelation of a Power higher than the world, which is manifested in nature and attested by conscience.

The Scriptures everywhere assume that God manifests Himself in nature. This is evident in the entire Old Testament, especially in the Psalms and Job. This self-disclosing of God in nature is referred to as a familiar thing by Jesus, as when He says: "Behold the birds" etc., Mt 6:26.

St. Paul repeatedly appeals to it, especially when preaching to the Gentiles, Act 14:17; 17:24; Ro 1:19-20.

The fact of conscience, which attests the moral government of God, is abundantly confirmed in the Bible, especially in the New Testament, where the name first appears. The heathen are called to repentance just like the Jews, Lu. 24:47; Act 17:30. The possession of moral consciousness is attributed to those who have not the Mosaic law, Rom 1:32; 2:15. A striking instance of its manifestation is Felix, Act 24:25.

This revelation of God, which the Bible assumes inadequate to be universal, has been so corrupted by sin in men that it does not furnish an adequate knowledge of what God is. It may be said the heathen know what God is, but not who He is. In the proposition, "This is God," they have the idea of the predicate "God", but they do not know the subject "This." Who "This" is they are ignorant of. In this sense the heathen are said to be without God, Eph 2:12, and to come to the knowledge of God through the Gospel, Gal 4:8-9.

The knowledge of God by natural revelation, however blurred, is of supreme importance in the history of salvation. It is an evidence of the redeemability of man. The supernatural saving knowledge of God forms connection with it. If man did not possess conscience and natural knowledge of God, it is difficult to see where grace would lay hold of him for redemption. No race of man has been found without it. Our old theologians rightly ascribed to it a "pedagogic" value, thus paralleling it with the law as a tutor to Christ.

The natural revelation of God suggests the so-called proofs for the existence of God. The validity of these proofs has often been called in question. This is not the place to discuss the worth of these arguments. We freely admit that they do not demonstrate the existence of God. But they confirm the faith in such existence. They have the value of corroborations of the scriptural assumption that belief in God is natural to man. The chief of these proofs are the ontological, cosmological, teleological, historical and moral arguments.

Their history is briefly this. They originated in Greek philosophy; were adopted by patristic theology, notably by Augustine; were more fully elaborated by the scholastics of the Middle Ages, especially by Anselm and Thomas Aquinas; were taken up by the orthodox theology of the seventeenth century; were revised by modern philosophy from Descartes down; and have been more or less recognized by modern theology.

THE SUPERNATURAL REVELATION OF GOD.

God has revealed Himself as a personal being, who stands in living relations to men. He has done this through chosen agents, to whom He manifested Himself by deed and word, and finally in direct personal manifestation in Jesus Christ.

The special feature in the conception of the supernatural revelation of God is the prominence given to His personality. He is not only an intelligent being, but also a moral and spiritual personality. He makes fellowship with Himself possible to man.

He has made Himself so known as a living person to chosen agents and through them to others. The idea now widely prevails that the real revelation of God is in every man's consciousness, and that the chosen instruments, referred to in the Bible, only had a stronger and more vivid experience of the common human consciousness of God. This is a perversion of the idea of revelation, which in the true sense means that God has made Himself known by some activity. The agents upon whom and through whom He worked were sometimes an entire people, as Israel at Sinai, sometimes chosen individuals, whom the Scriptures call prophets and apostles. The revelation in Christ was unique, for He was not an agent of God, but the incarnation of God.

The revelation of God was by deed and word. The word must not be construed as merely man's explanation of the acts of God. Nor must the revelation of God be limited to the word, as if it were merely indoctrination. Older Protestant theology was inclined to this misconception. The word accompanies the acts as their interpretation, and afterwards abides, in the written form to which it was reduced, as the authentic record of the revelation.

The history contained in the Bible shows that God's revelation was progressive. It developed according to the needs, condition and receptivity of men. The New Testament looks back upon this progress in God's revelation and distinctly asserts it, Heb 1:1, 2; 2 Co 3:6; Eph 3:5.

The old question as to the relation of reason to revelation calls for a few remarks. The vital point is really as to the seat of authority, which has already been discussed. Revelation is not a supplement to reason nor a substitute for it in obtaining knowledge of God. The data of revelation come before the mind like other data of life for thoughtful appropriation and appreciation. The truth concerning God and His redemptive works is not given through reason, but it is apprehended by reason as the faculty of understanding in man. Like other data of life, and even more than they, the data of revelation may find hindrances in the condition of man which prevent their appropriation. The Scriptures refer to the hindrances to the believing acceptance of revelation which sin causes, 1 Co 1:22, 23; 2:14; 2 Co 10:5.

It is not necessary to prove the possibility, necessity, reality and truth of supernatural revelation to Christian faith. Such questions belong to apologetics and not to dogmatics. The possibility lies in the freedom of God, which cannot be restricted by a necessitarian conception of the immutablity of God, such as pantheists hold, nor by an unalterable order of the world as a system of laws, such as deists maintain. The necessity springs from the sinful condition of man and his need of redemption, which deists and rationalists in vain seek to minimize. The reality is a matter of fact and so of historical proof. A naturalistic explanation of Jesus Christ and of the entire history of the Bible is impossible. The truth of a supernatural revelation can only be grasped by religious experience. Rational arguments may silence objections; they cannot produce faith. Conviction of the truth of revelation is a divine work in the soul through the revelation.

This leads up to what is called the testimony of the Holy Spirit. Christ said that the Spirit of truth, who proceeds from the Father, should bear witness of Himself. St. Paul declares of himself and other believers: "We received, not the spirit of the world, but the Spirit which is from God, that we might know the things that were freely given to us of God." 1 Co 2:12. This testimony of the Holy Spirit is a matter of inward experience, but it is not merely subjective. There is in it an application of the principle of causality. He whom the truth of God's revelation has made free, knows by his experience what kind of action upon his heart has liberated him, namely the truth and action of the Holy Spirit. This testimony is properly regarded as the ultimate ground of certitude in regard to God's Word.

THE NATURE OF GOD.

God is a person, who in Himself is perfect life, and whose essential character is love.

The possibility of defining God has from the early ages of the Church been questioned. But the doubt has always been suggested by abstract philosophical considerations, and not by the representation of God in the Bible. Of course the logical categories of genus and species are inapplicable here. But the Christian has a distinct conception of God, whom he worships, to whom he prays, and in whose fellowship he lives. Nor is this merely a subjective idea without corresponding objective reality. God has truly revealed Himself. As surely as there is a revelation of God, He can be defined.

The Christian conception of God is not formed from reflections upon pure being, abstract, ultimate, absolute. It is obtained from God's manifestation of Himself in personal life. The definition of God should therefore combine those most essential characteristics, which are exhibited in the revelation that God has given of Himself. There are three such characteristics indicated in the Scriptures: first, perfect self-conscious will; second, perfect moral character; third, perfect self-sufficiency and independence. The first characteristic is manifested in that God reveals Himself as a person; the second in that He reveals Himself as love; the third in that He reveals Himself as life.

The Bible contains no theory of God's essence. It presents Him in living activity. It lies in the nature of a progressive revelation that in the course of God's dealings with mankind, the idea of God should become more distinct, purer, richer, more spiritual. From the beginning the Old Testament contains the truth of ethical monotheism, although in patriarchal and early Israelite history this monotheism is implied rather than defined. At first Jehovah is known as Israel's God. Only in the course of His dealings with Israel is the full truth emphasized that He is the only God, that He rules all nations and the entire world, and that He is holy love. It was not till the age of the prophets that the nature and character of Jehovah were explicitly opposed to the false gods who are vanity. This historical fact is overstrained by many biblical critics and converted into the theory that ethical monotheism originated in Israel with the prophets of a later period.

No certain inference as to the idea of God can be made from the etymology of the Hebrew names for God. But the historical use of these names is suggestive. The two chief names are Elohim and Jehovah. Elohim is used in connections that indicate God's dominion over the world. Whether the derivation from El, meaning the Strong, is correct or not, Elohim is the almighty Ruler of the universe. Jehovah is the covenant God of Israel. The explanation of the name in Ex 3:14, "I am that I am," is significative rather than etymological. It does not denote unconditional being, but, concretely, unchangeableness in covenant relations, faithfulness.

The representation of God in the Old Testament makes prominent the idea that God is a person, that He is the source of all life and Himself perfect life, and that His nature is love and holiness. His holiness is much stressed. In Isaiah the special name of Jehovah is the Holy One of Israel. The superiority of the religion of Israel over heathen religions is nowhere more manifest than in its moral and spiritual' conception of God, and this is a striking proof of the revealed character of that religion.

The spiritual conception of God in the Old Testament is carried forward to complete expression in the New Testament. The characteristic designation for God by Jesus is Father, and in the epistles "the Father of our Lord Jesus Christ." The special work of God described in the New Testament is redemption from sin. In it God manifests Himself as love, so that St. John can say: "God is love." 1 Jn 4:8. God also reveals Himself as the power of redemption. As vital energy, which quickens and brings men into fellowship with Himself, God is life, eternal life, 1 Jn 5:20 ; Jn 5 :26 ; Lu 20:38. The term "spirit" in Jn 4:24 implies the same truth, for it is the spirit that gives life, Jn 6:63. In redeeming mankind from sin on moral terms God is revealed in His holiness, 1 P 1:16, a characteristic elsewhere expressed by the term light, 1 Jn 1 :5, 1 Tim 6 :16. In short, the New Testament conception of God is that of a perfect personal Father, who is the fullness of life and from whom all life comes, and whose essential characteristic is holy love.

THE ATTRIBUTES OF GOD.

The essence of God is manifested to us in His attributes, which we derive from the various aspects and relations of His activity toward the world and His revelation to us.

The attributes are the distinguishing characteristics of God which underlie His various manifestations. They are not variable qualities, which can be thought away and God still be what He is, for they inhere in the essence of God. Are the attributes of God merely forms of our thinking of Him or are they actually existent in Him? This is an old question, which has been differently answered. All agree that the attributes are inadequate expressions of the fullness of life, perfection and majesty in God. The subjective view, that the attributes are merely differences in the human conception of God, was maintained by Augustine, by the Nominalists of the medieval period (who said they were only a distinction in names) and in a peculiar way by Schleiermacher. The objective view, that something real in God corresponds to the attributes, was taught by Thomas Aquinas and afterwards by Post-reformation theology generally. There are differences in the objective view, some regarding the attributes as modes of revelation with a corresponding background in God; others regarding them as internal differentiations in the being of God, as when Thomasius says: "Divine attributes are the immanent determinations of the absolute personality in relation to Himself." Similarly Frank says: "They must constitute and characterize the divine essence, if they really are divine attributes."

This latter view that the attributes represent internal differentiations in God is hardly tenable. Their distinction belongs to the revelation of God. This question is related to another question, namely, What is the relation of the attributes to the essence of God? They are certainly not parts of God, as if He were composite. Theology has always emphasized the simplicity of God's being. On the other hand, it is too much to say with John Damascenus, that the attributes do not denote the essence of God, but only relations or activities of God. Augustine laid down a proposition, which afterwards dominated Scholasticism and orthodox Protestant theology, namely: "In God essence and attributes are one." Seventeenth century theology maintained, correctly we believe, that the attributes are not really, but formally according to our mode of conception, distinguished from the divine essence.

The simplest and the most widely accepted classification of the divine attributes divide them into two groups: immanent and relative. The immanent attributes characterize God considered in Himself, relations to the world being abstracted. It must not be overlooked that these attributes are known to us only by God's operations in the world. But attention is fixed upon God apart from and in contrast with the world. The immanent attributes are: self - existence (also called aseity and independence), life, eternity, immutability, infinity, unity (simplicity), spirituality.

The relative attributes are ascribed to God with regard to His relations to the world. The world is considered in two aspects: as the sphere of space and time, and as the sphere of a moral order. The relative attributes are subdivided accordingly. Attributes in relation to the world of space and time: omnipresence, omnipotence, omniscience, wisdom. Attributes in relation to the moral world: under the concept of love as a fundamental characteristic of God's being, faithfulness, grace, mercy, patience, benignity (goodness); under the concept of holiness as a fundamental characteristic of God's being, righteousness, truth.

Writers on dogmatics are wont to define and discuss these attributes singly. In a brief outline like this it is not necessary to do so. It may be assumed that the concepts signified by the terms used are generally understood. But it is proper to direct the attention of the student to some difficult questions connected with the attributes of God. For the most part these questions arise from the difficulty of conceiving at the same time a real history of the world in space and time, with mutations and contingencies, and the absoluteness of God. The eternity of God implies that He is independent of all changes of time, and yet in creation and redemption He works in time. The difficulty is that God seems to be in some way subject to time, which His eternity forbids. Again, God's omnipotence seems to conflict with freedom in created personalities. Again, God's omniscience is difficult to harmonize with future contingencies and with self-determinations of free creatures. No attempt will be made here to solve these difficulties. The general question of the relation of the finite to the infinite is beyond the comprehension of the human mind. Scripture faith requires us to hold fast to the reality of the world's history and the reality of God's attributes. No explanation of these problems that infringes upon either side can be correct.

THE TRINITY.

The revelation of God, viewed in its entirety, embraces three inseparably connected operations: the creation of the world, the redemption of mankind through Christ, and the renewal of mankind in fellowship with God by the Holy Spirit. The one God manifests Himself in threefoldness. There are three to whom divine names, attributes, works and worship are ascribed, and yet there is no division or separation in God. This truth has been formulated by the Church in the doctrine of the Trinity, namely, that God, one in essence, subsists in three persons.

The salvation of mankind is based upon the revelation which God has made of Himself as Father, Son and Holy Spirit. Much speculation has been expended upon the development of the doctrine of the Trinity, but the doctrine is not a mere matter of speculative interest. The vital truth of salvation is bound up in it.

In considering the scriptural statements concerning Father, Son and Holy Spirit, a theological distinction should be borne in mind between an economic and an immanent Trinity. The term economic, derived from ancient Church usage, refers to the separate historical manifestations of God. Historically God is brought into view as Father, Son and Holy Spirit. There is a distinction of revelation of the three. This is an economic Trinity. But now the question arises, whether there are in the being of God distinctions, which correspond with the differences of manifestation and which underlie them. The language of Scripture itself refers back to ontological distinctions between Father, Son and Spirit. The Church is therefore justified in regarding the distinctions in the Trinity as immanent. The Scriptures teach not only historical manifestations of Father, Son and Holy Spirit, but also the preexistence of each of these. The distinction between them is preexistent, and if preexistent, eternal. For the Church, in its early wrestling with this problem, correctly perceived that if a beginning is assigned to the personal distinction between the three, the Son and Spirit must be degraded to the level of creatures.

The proof of the Trinity from Scripture cannot ignore the progress of revelation. A proposition of Calixtus in the seventeenth century, which was much opposed by the orthodox theologians of that age, is no longer questioned, namely, that the doctrine of the Trinity is taught only implicitly, not explicitly in the Old Testament. For this reason, in collecting the scriptural evidence for the Trinity, it is best to begin at the summit of revelation in the New Testament, and from there consider the foreshadowing in the Old Testament.

The method of proof, that shall be followed here, is to show first the divinity of the three persons separately, and then to show their unity.

The divinity of the Father lies in the very conception of God. It needs no further argumentation. For the Scriptures so identify the Father of our Lord Jesus Christ with God that there can be no question that what is ascribed to God belongs to the Father. The only question can be whether like divinity is ascribed to the Son and Holy Spirit. The divinity of the Son is proved from the New Testament first by the testimony of Jesus Himself, and then by the testimony of the apostles and other witnesses.

The testimony of Jesus Himself includes the following particulars:

1. He claims a unique relation to God as His Father. So in the synoptic gospels, Mt 11:27; 16:27; 26:63, and parallel passages. So especially throughout the gospel of St. John, 5:17; 5:26; 10:38; 14:9; 20:17, etc.

2. He claims preexistence for Himself, Jn 6:38; 8:42, 58; 16:28; 17:5.

3. He claims divine attributes and prerogatives. He claims the power to forgive sins, Mt 9:6; of judgment, Mt 25:31; the attribute of eternity, Mt 28:20. So in John He claims all judgment, 5:22; life, 5:26 ; the hearing of prayer, 14:13.

4. He calls Himself the Son of God. It may be conceded that in some passages this designation is used in the

sense of a theocratic mission and is equivalent to Messiah, as in Lu 4:41 and even in Mt 16:16; cf. the parallels in Mk 8:29; Lu 9:20. But nothing less than a unique personal relation, involving unity of essence, is implied in Mt 11:27 and throughout the gospel of John.

The testimony of the apostles shows that to them Jesus was nothing less than God incarnate.

1. He is called the Son of God, and this in an ontological sense, Ro 1:3, 4 ; 8:3; Gal 4 :4 ; Heb 1 :2.

2. He is called God, Jn 20:28; Ro 9:5; Tit 2:13; Heb 1:8; 1 Jn 5:20.

3. The fullness of the Godhead is ascribed to Him, Col 2:9.

4. Preexistence and creative activity are ascribed to Him, Jn 1:1; 1 Co 8:6; Col 1:15, 16; Heb 1:2, 10.

5. Prayer is addressed to Him, Act 7:59; 9:13; 1 Co 1 :2 ; 2 Co 12 :8.

6. He is regularly named Lord in the New Testament in the sense of the Old Testament Jehovah.

7. The titles, Word and image of God, are applied to Him in a way to express an essential relation to God and not merely historical manifestation, Jn 1:1; 2 Co 4:4; Col 1:15; Heb 1:3.

The proof for the place of the Holy Spirit in the Godhead necessarily deals more with the evidence for the distinct personality of the Spirit than for His divinity. For there can be no question that the New Testament carries over the Old Testament conception of the Spirit as the divine energy of life, or, as Davidson expresses it, 'God efficient, God in operation."

1. The distinct personality of the Spirit is declared by Jesus in the promise of the Comforter, who does personal

acts, speaks, teaches, leads into truth, convicts and bears witness, Jn 14:16, 26; 15:26; 16:8, 13. Of special significance is the circumstance that, while the Greek word for spirit is neuter, Jesus refers to Him with the masculine pronoun. In like manner the apostles everywhere speak of the Spirit as personal, Ro 8:16, 26; Eph 4:30; Rev 22:17.

2. Personal divine authority and majesty are ascribed to the Spirit by Jesus. Cf. Mt 12:31 and parallels in Mk and Lu. So also by the apostles: 1 Co 3:16; Heb 10:29.

3. Procession from the Father and the Son is declared of the Spirit by Jesus, Jn 14:26; 15:26. Also by St. Peter, Act 2:17, 33. Modern exegesis refers such passages to the historical manifestation of the Spirit and not, as was formerly done, to the eternal procession. We accept the modern exegesis, but at the same time we recognize that the historical mission of the Spirit presupposes an internal relation to those who send Him.

4. The Holy Spirit is called God, Act 5:3-4.

5. Divine works and attributes are ascribed to the Spirit by Jesus, Mt 12:28, Jn 16:8; and still more explicitly by the apostles, Ro 8:11; 1 Co 2:10 ; 12 :8 ; 1 P 1 :11. The works of grace by which men are renewed unto life in God, are attributed to the Spirit by Jesus as well as the apostles: regeneration, Jn 3:5; Tit 3:5; sanctification, Ro 15:16; 2 Thess 2:13; 1 Pet 1:2; hope, Rom 15:13; faith, Gal 3:2; new life in God generally, 1 Co 6:11.

A few passages require special notice because they present difficulties. In Jn 7:39 the Spirit is spoken of as if He had a beginning. The allusion is doubtless to Pentecost. The difficulty is solved if we understand the reference to the Spirit as "not yet" of His manifestation as the Spirit sent by Christ, and not of His existence. In Ro 8:9, 10 and 2 Co 3:17 there is an apparent identification of the Spirit with Christ. The apparent identity is one of gracious operation, not of person. The grace of Christ is mediated by the Spirit.

The divinity of the Father, of the Son, and of the Holy Spirit being proved from the New Testament, it remains to consider the relation of the three to each other. That relation involves both a coordination and a subordination.

1. The three are coordinated so as to imply unity and equality, Mt 28:19; 2 Co 13:14. Here also belong those combinations and alternations of the three in the work of divine grace, which imply unity and equality, Ro 8:11; 1 Co 12:4-6; Eph 4:4-6; Jude 20, 21.

2. There is a manifest subordination of the Son to the Father, Jn 5:19; 8:28; 14:28; 20:17; 1 Co 11:3; 15:28. This subordination is not in conflict with the coordination just noted, for it is manifestly one of function in the work of redemption, and not of essential being. Similarly a subordination of the Spirit to the Father and to the Son is implied in all that is said of His being sent by the Father through the Son. This is also a matter of redemptive office, not of essence.

The Old Testament, in keeping with its character as a preparatory revelation, contains only anticipations of the full truth of the Trinity. Such anticipations in regard to the Son are to be found in the theophanies as the Angel of Jehovah, Gen 16:7; 21:17; 22:11; in the making of the Wisdom of God personal, Prov 8:22; more distinctly in the coming of Jehovah in the predicted time of redemption, Is 60:1; Mi 4:7; Mal 3:1; especially in the prophecy of the Messiah as a divine person, Is 9:6; 11:1; Mi 5:2; and His designation as the Son of God, Ps 2:7, and as Lord, Ps 110:1, Jer 23:6.

As to the Spirit in the Old Testament, divine effects of the most varied character are ascribed to the Spirit of God: in the cosmic sphere, Gen 1:2; Ps 33:6; 104:30; in the life of man, Ex 31:3; Num 11:29; in the minds of men, especially as the power of prophecy; also in the inner life of the soul, Ps 51:11. The future outpouring of the Spirit is predicted, Joel 2:28; Is 44:3, and that as the principle of new spiritual life, Ez 36:27. In all of these manifestations the Spirit is on the one hand identified with God, on the other differentiated from Him. Whatever is effected by the Spirit is God's own work, and yet the Spirit is distinguished from God as His power, in one place almost, though not fully, personalized, Is 48:16. A coordination of three persons is not found in the Old Testament, the proof of older theologians for such coordination from the plural form of Elohim, from passages where God speaks in the plural, from the benediction, Num 6:24, and from the threefold repetition of Holy, Is 6:3, being forced and inadequate.

The development of the doctrine of the Trinity in the early Church attained its culmination in the Nicene Creed and its completion in Augustine. The development was directed at first by opposition to Monarchianism, the assertion that God was one person, in the forms of Dynamism and Modalism, according to the former of which Christ was only a man endowed with supernatural powers, according to the latter of which God passed through three successive modes of manifestation. The latter doctrine is also called Sabellianism. Afterwards the development was directed by opposition to Arianism, which made of Christ a created intermediate being, who existed before the world, and of the Holy Spirit an impersonal power. In the Nicene Creed the Spirit was said to proceed "from the Father." In the West under the influence of Augustine "and from the Son" was added.

The old Lutheran dogmaticians carefully systematized the doctrine, for the most part using formulas and distinctions worked out by earlier writers. Their scheme is helpful to categorize ideas on this important subject. Therefore it is presented here in outline according to Baier. Essence and all divine perfections are common to the three, whom the Scriptures call Father, Son and Holy Spirit. Among these three there is no substantial difference. Each is true and eternal God. They are not three gods, but one God. In order to exclude heresies the ancient Church declared that there are three persons or hypostases in one essence. The essence is the divine nature. The persons are three subsistences. They are distinguished by personal acts, properties and notions. The personal acts are two: the generation of the Son and the spiration of the Holy Spirit. These personal acts are within the divine essence and are called *opera ad intra*. As such they are distinguished from the outward works, called *opera ad extra*, namely, creation, redemption and sanctification. The latter are defined as undivided, because they are acts of the whole Godhead, although in each of them one person is especially manifested. The inward works, *opera ad intra*, are divided, proceeding from person to person. The personal properties are three: paternity (in the Father), filiation (in the Son), procession (in the Holy Spirit). The personal notions are two: unbegottenness (belonging to the Father) and active spiration (belonging to the Father and the Son). According to these distinctions each of the three persons and also the whole Godhead are separately defined. It is not necessary to repeat the separate definitions.

Modern constructions of the Trinity have largely been
formulations of a process in the absolute Being under the
influence of speculative philosophy, or a reverting to
Sabellianizing conceptions as in Schleiermacher, or tending
towards Unitarianism with a recognition of something divine
in Christ and the Holy Spirit. Antitrinitarian views, such as
arose in the early Church, revived in the time of the
Reformation and crystallized in the Unitarianism of
Socinianism. In the eighteenth century Rationalism
undermined the doctrine of the Trinity and Unitarianism
spread in England and the United States.

To grasp the truth of the Trinity the proper method is
to begin with the facts of God's revelation and rise by
necessary inference from them to the being of God itself.
God is creator and upholder of the world. Jesus Christ is the
redeemer of the world and as such is revealed as the Son of
God, and in Him God is revealed as the Father of this Son.
The Holy Spirit is the giver of life in the world and as such is
revealed as a divine person, who is the Spirit of God and of
Christ. Distinguished as each of these three is from the
others, and existing as they do in personal relations to each
other, nevertheless the same divine life is in all. As this is so
in the manifestation in this world by creation, redemption
and sanctification, it must be so in the life of God as such,
that is, eternally. For what is in God does not become; it is.
Trinity belongs to the very personal life of God. Frank has
expressed this sequence of ideas in the following terms:

"In the experience of salvation and according to the
Scriptures the working of the living, absolute God has
everywhere proved itself to be personal, and therefore
personality belongs to the absolute God as such and

in His self-existence. But this same personality has disclosed itself in the course of the history of revelation and for the consciousness of salvation conditioned thereby, as working in the form of a threefold 'I,' and for this reason it must itself be conceived as existing in a threefold hypostasis, in the self-distinction and contraposition of the Father and of the Son and of the Holy Spirit."

CHAPTER II
THE WORLD AND MAN

THE COMMUNION OF MAN WITH GOD ESTABLISHED IN THE CREATION OF THE WORLD AND MAN

CREATION:

The relations of God to mankind are determined by the act of creation. Man by his nature is fitted for a moral and spiritual life, and the world by its nature is suitably ordered to be the scene of such life. Herein lies the religious significance of creation. In it God revealed His love, the same love that impelled Him to redeem man when union with God was broken by sin. As an act of God and not a process in Him or in independently existent matter, creation is an absolutely originating act, bringing the universe into being out of nothing. As an act of love creation is a free act of God. Hence it is declared by the Bible to be by the Word of God.

The scriptural doctrine of creation must be derived from both the Old and New Testament. For the connection of creation with redemption and with the perfecting of the kingdom of God must be observed in the Christian point of view. The preexistent Redeemer is both the mediator and goal of creation: Jn 1:3; 1 Co 8:6; Col 1:16; Heb 1:2. In our older theology we find the idea of the Trinity correctly introduced into creation. As an *opus ad extra* creation is a work of the entire Trinity, although by appropriation referred especially to the Father. That creation is the work of the Father needs no proof. That the Son is mediator and end of creation is proved by the passages just referred to. The connection of the Holy Spirit with creation lies in the general conception that He is the giver of life, Jn 6:63; 2 Co 3:6. Moreover creation is expressly ascribed to the Spirit: Gen 1:2; Ps 33:6; Job 33:4.

There is a double account of the work of creation in the first two chapters of Genesis. Modern criticism generally claims that the two are discordant. But there is no contradiction. The first is an account of the origin of the world; the second of the preparation of the earth as a habitation for man. In these accounts four fundamental religious truths are revealed: the monotheistic conception of God; the origin of the world by the will of God; the teleological progress up to man as the head of created beings; the destiny of man for communion with God. These fundamentals pervade the whole Bible and are implied in other references to creation, Ps 33:6; 90:2; 104:5; Job 38:4; Act 17:24: Ro 11:36; Heb 11:8.

The succession of six days of creative activity belongs to the mode and not to the essence of creation. Attempts to harmonize the six days with science have no significance for dogmatics, however satisfying they may be to the Christian student of modern science. More important are the relations of the scriptural view of creation to philosophical opinions. When the Bible represents creation as an effect produced by the Word of God, it declares that it was the free, conscious act of divine will. This excludes all ideas of the origin of the world by an emanation from God, or by a pantheistic process of God unfolding Himself in the world, or by an evolution of eternally existing matter. The existence of God must in no way be conditioned by the world. Creation is not a necessary act; it is the act of free love and as such includes also the revelation of the divine love which redeems the world. Creation by the Word of God puts the created universe outside of the being of God, but it does not make it independent of Him. On the contrary it implies that the same Word ever upholds it. In relation to the world which He has made, God is both transcendent and immanent.

The biblical teaching of creation out of nothing excludes the idea of the eternity of matter. For creation is not merely the arrangement of preexistent matter, but the origination of matter and its arrangement. Materialism is absolutely to be rejected, and with it that form of evolution which is materialistic. However, it is not inconsistent with the scriptural doctrine of creation to recognize an evolution within the created world, by which the divine idea is gradually realized and higher forms of creatures arise out of lower forms under the direction of God.[2]

Creation looks to a goal. This goal is inseparable creation from the central and dominating position of man in creation. In the first chapter of Genesis the creative works of God reach their end when God created man in His own image; and in the second chapter man is the center of all the creative activity described. It is not claimed that other creatures exist merely for man. They are ends in themselves. But the purposes realized in them are relative to the purpose of the whole creation, and this purpose centers in man. Creation looks towards the Kingdom of God, and in that Kingdom the destiny of man is primary. It furnishes the key

---

[2] This statement should not be seen as an absolute acceptance of Theistic evolution. Though Voigt allows for the evolution of creation in some sense, he later explicitly denies the evolution of humankind from another form as contradictory to the Biblical testimony that man is a unique creation of God.

to the meaning of the whole course of the world. It is this truth that gives significance to the doctrine of the cosmic position of Christ, upon which St. Paul dwells in Ephesians and Colossians when he explains the universal scope of God's purpose of redemption.

PROVIDENCE.

By providence is meant the activity of God upon and in the world, by which its existence is perpetuated and its course directed so that the divine purpose is realized in it. In the providential activity of God preservation and government are usually distinguished.

In Christianity providence cannot be separated from the divine purpose of salvation. This purpose runs through the whole activity of God in relation to the world, for it is an eternal purpose, Eph 1:4; 3:11. The order of nature and the order of grace may be distinguished, but they must not be separated.

That so elementary a religious truth as the providence of God is found everywhere in the Bible needs no remark. However, we are so accustomed to think of second causes and natural laws that we often fail to apprehend the intensity of the sense of God's presence and activity in the world, which finds expression in the Scriptures. The following quotation from A. B. Davidson with reference to the Old Testament will be helpful in getting nearer to it:

> "Two beliefs characterize the Hebrew mind from the beginning: first, the strong belief in causation — every change on the face of nature, or in the life of men or nations, must be due to a cause; and,

secondly, the only conceivable causality is a personal agent. The unseen power under all things, which threw up all changes on the face of the world, which gave animation to the creature or withdrew it, which moved the generations of men upon the earth from the beginning (Is 41:4) — was the living God. Some phenomena or events, such as the thunder storm or the dividing of the sea, might be more striking instances of His operation than others. They were miracles, that is, wonders, but they did not differ in kind from the ordinary phenomena of nature, from His making the sun to rise and sealing up the stars (Job 9:7), from His clothing the heavens with blackness (Is 50:3) and making them clear again with His breath (Job 26:13). Everything is supernatural, that is, direct divine operation."

The New Testament conception does not differ from this view, except that Jesus makes a more immediate application of providence to individual believers, and St. Paul combines the course of God's providential operations with His grand work of redemption.

The connection of providence with redemption illumines the problem of evil. The principle of retribution, that God rewards the good and punishes the wicked in this world, pervades the Old Testament. But it was often felt that the principle appeared to disagree with actual experience. It fails to meet the case of undeserved suffering. Therefore already in the Old Testament, especially in Job, some evils are viewed as disciplinary, and in Isaiah, chapter 53, sufferings are shown to be redemptive. In the New Testament the revelation of the love of God in Christ makes the painful leadings of providence appear as an exercise of the faith of His children and removes their sting by the promise that ultimately all evils shall be abolished for the redeemed. Because there is redemption, there is good even in the evils which believers suffer.

It is an old theological notion that providence is a continued creation. As opposed to a deistic conception that the world runs by itself without further intervention of God, it contains an important truth. But it is a one-sided view, virtually denying the existence of permanent forces in the created world. The world is not being brought into existence anew every moment. Genesis says, "The heaven and the earth were finished." But the continued existence of the world is founded upon the working of God. This upholding activity of God is both transcendent and immanent. If the immanence of God is denied, the world is made independent of God— the deistic error. If the transcendence of God is denied, God and the world are confused—the pantheistic error. Providence is an activity of God within the world from without.

The distinction between a general, special and most special providence is formal. It must not suggest that God is more indifferent to some creatures than others. He cares for each according to its kind. The real intent of this distinction is to classify the objects of providence qualitatively: first, creatures generally; secondly, men; thirdly, the godly.

The form in which providence is exercised is twofold: preservation and government. Involved in both is the idea of concurrence, the conception that an operation of God underlies all that comes to pass.

Preservation is the name for the sustaining activity of God. This activity needs to be insisted on to oppose the deistic idea, which derives so much strength from modern science, that the continuance of the world is simply dependent upon the forces introduced into creation at the beginning. Undoubtedly there are powers of continuity and development in things created. But the world exists not only by an original fiat of the Creator, but also by the continuous working of God's power. If God withdraws His power, things perish, as is beautifully said in Ps 104:29: "Thou hidest thy face, they are troubled; thou takest away their breath, they die and return to their dust." Providence is not simply provision, but continuous cooperation.

Government is that activity of God by which the existence and action of all things are directed to the accomplishment of God's purposes. It is the expression of a divine teleology in the universe. The government of God must not be identified with the laws of nature, although those laws are the normal lines along which it works. But God's government is free activity, upon which the order of the operation of the various energies in the universe, physical and spiritual, depends. The truth of a divine purpose excludes the error of chance, just as the truth of the freedom of God's government excludes the error of fatalism. In the freedom of God's government of the world lies the possibility of free rational creatures. Because God governs all things with freedom and intelligence and not by necessity, He can make room in the universe for the action of free, intelligent creatures. For this reason He can also hear and answer prayer.

The traditional analysis of God's government into four lines of control, by: permission, hindrance, direction and limitation, is practical and somewhat mechanical. It contributes little to the understanding of the problems involved in the relation of God to things, events and actions.

In the true sense God can never be in an attitude of mere permission or mere hindrance. As He is causative in the direction and termination of events, so is He also in what we call permission and hindrance. That the forces in the world, physical, vital, mental and moral, lead to such results as they do, is due ultimately to the divine causality, which sustains and governs all secondary causality to the extent to which it operates. In all that comes to pass the devout mind sees the hand of God. As has been shown, this is the teaching of the Old Testament and the New.

The activity of God even in the minutest circumstances of life is impressively expressed by our Lord: "Are not two sparrows sold for a farthing? and not one of them shall fall on the ground without your Father: but the very hairs of your head are all numbered," Mt 10:29 Theologically this is called concurrence. Concurrence with all movements and actions in the universe cannot be rightly conceived, if the purpose of God that runs through all from creation to the consummation of the Kingdom of God is left out of view. For the divine concurrence is not the operation of an invisible omnipresent force among other forces. It is a personal concurrence. God acts as an intelligent and moral being when He preserves the world and directs its course. As the deistic notion that God no longer interposes in the world, which He has wisely ordered, must be rejected, so also the deterministic idea that the movement of every atom, the operation of every force, the spring of every impulse and the rise of every thought, are unalterably fixed beforehand.

When it is borne in mind that God's concurrence is not physical force, but personal direction and cooperation, it is easier to deal with the difficult question of God's concurrence with moral acts of created beings. It is not so difficult to see that God actively promotes the morally good. But it is difficult to understand His concurrence with the morally bad. There is danger here of compromising His moral nature. The old scholastic distinction that in such acts God concurs with the effects but not in the defects, in the operation, but not in the evil quality of the act, is true and useful as far as it goes. But it does not go to the root of the difficulty, for God still seems to aid the evil deed. How can He have any part at all in operations evilly designed and executed? The answer must be found in the view which we take of God's purpose that determines His concurrence. God does not produce moral evil. But when it arises, God also takes it up into His purpose. "He makes the wrath of man to praise Him." In ruling and overruling sin, He causes sin to work out its proper results, so that sin shall earn its wages, death; and He concurs to the end that where sin has abounded, grace shall much more abound. Similarly the sufferings of the righteous and innocent by the sins of the wicked are controlled by God for the fulfillment of His moral purpose in regard to both the righteous and the wicked.

MIRACLES

Miracles are extraordinary manifestations of providence, that is, of God's interposition in the course of the world's events. They belong to the sphere of redemption and are inseparable from it. The possibility of miracles is based on the freedom of God, their necessity upon the salvation of mankind, and their reality upon facts recorded in the history of God's revelation.

That the Bible records events which were designed to be regarded as miracles is indisputable. Christian belief in miracles is simply a matter of accepting the authentic record of God's revelation. In the New Testament they are called by different names: powers, with reference to the power of God manifested in them; wonders, with reference to their effect upon the human mind; signs, with reference to their significance. For the latter two there are corresponding names in the Old Testament. An easy way to dispose of the reality of the miracles in the Bible is to assert that the ancients knew nothing of natural law. Undoubtedly they had not the conception of the reign of law, which modern science teaches. They may have sometimes confused the miraculous with the unusual. Even now many try to identify the two and regard a miracle merely as an occurrence, the laws of which are not understood. But it is not a question of what the ancient idea of natural law or miracle was. We have the record of what occurred and many of these occurrences, if the record of them is accepted at all, must be classed as miracles.

The religious question involved here is whether God manifested Himself so specially, with or without the operation of ordinary natural forces, that the work of establishing His Kingdom was advanced by it. For miracles must not be regarded as isolated occurrences in the history of the world, but as forming an essential part of that historical revelation of God, culminating in the miraculous person of Jesus Christ, through which the salvation of man from moral evil and its consequences is brought about. Miracles belong to the sphere of redemption and are inseparable from it.

Two classes of scriptural miracles may be distinguished: those by which the redemptive purpose of God was objectively advanced, and those by which faith was strengthened and so progress was made subjectively for

God's revelation. Instances of the former are the exodus of Israel from Egypt, the incarnation and the resurrection of our Lord. An instance of the faith-producing sign was the miracle at Cana, of which St. John says: "Jesus manifested His glory and His disciples believed on Him," Jn 2:11.

To the modern mind the difficulty in the possibility of miracle lies in the apparent conflict with natural law. But religion may not unreasonably demand that, whatever use science may make of its conception of natural law in its own sphere, there are realms of being to which it does not apply, and especially is this true of the field of divine revelation that religion takes cognizance of. If God is indeed restricted by what science conceives to be laws of nature, He is incapable of performing miracles. But such a god would be incapable of governing the world. God is free; when His wisdom demands it, He introduces something new into the world. An additional operation of God out of the established course does not arrest or disturb nature. It is a notable fact that the scriptural miracles blend harmoniously with nature, which goes on in its course, the effects of the miracle conforming to its system. The fact of miracle has this great significance, that it exemplifies the divine teleology, which pursues redemptive ends in the history of the world.

ANGELS

As agencies of God's providential operations the Bible makes frequent mention of an order of intelligences outside of the order of this world. Their common name is angels, that is, messengers. Their nature is described as spirits, and their office as ministers and messengers of God. The Scriptures also refer to a class of spiritual beings who work evil.

They also are called angels, and a fall of them from the truth is mentioned. Hence the moral condition of angels is twofold, good and bad.

Our knowledge of angels is derived altogether from the Bible. For although we refer our protection in certain perils to guardian angels and our temptations to sin to evil spirits, we do so in belief of what we have learned from the Bible. We have no sensible experience of their presence now.

References to angels occur everywhere in the Bible. Besides the common name angel, they are called sons of God. The designations cherubim, seraphim, archangel are special, and appear not to apply to all. Two personal names occur: Gabriel and Michael. Together they constitute the heavenly host of God, surrounding His throne to do service. They accompany God when He executes judgment, and the Son of Man when He comes to judge. Ranks among them are indicated. Their office is to praise God, to execute His will, and to minister, as to Jesus in the wilderness and Gethsemane. They appear at all important epochs both in the Old and New Testament. The form of their appearance is that of men. Sometimes they have wings. Their nature is indicated by the designation, spirits, Heb 1:14. They are called the holy ones of God, but relatively to God they are imperfect, Job 4:18. Worship of them is condemned, Col 2:18; Rev 19:10. Moral differences exist among them.

In the Old Testament an angel is named, who is the adversary of God's people, Satan, 1 Chr 21:1; Job 1:6; Zech 3:1. The serpent mentioned in the story of Eden is first identified with Satan in the book of Wisdom, and then in Rev 12:9. The doctrine of Satan is more developed in the New Testament than the Old. That Jesus regarded the devil as a reality is proved by the story of His temptation as well as by other utterances, especially Jn 8:44. Jesus ascribes to the devil a retinue and a kingdom, Mt 25:41; 12:26. The angels were witnesses of creation, Job 38:7, but their own creation is nowhere described; nor is their fall, which is assumed in Jn 8:44; 1 Jn 3:8; Jude 6. A final judgment awaits them, Mt 25:41; 2 P 2:4; Rev 12:9; 20:10.

In nature angels are pure spirits, personal and finite. The office of the good angels is to adore God and to execute His commands. The work of evil angels is chiefly to tempt men to evil. A special form of their activity appears in demoniacal possession, which the New Testament by no means represents as merely aggravated physical or mental malady. Evil spirits are under the control of God's providence. The original moral state of all angels was good, with the possibility of sinning. Since the fall of some a division has ensued into those who are confirmed in holiness and those who are confirmed in wickedness beyond redemption.

The existence of angels was denied among the Jews by the Sadducees, Act 23:8, and in modern times by many skeptics. Where their existence has not been directly denied, it has often been attenuated to mere mythical or poetical conceptions or to ideal powers. But their activity is so closely interwoven with the facts of revelation that an earnest believer in the truth of the Bible cannot doubt their personal existence.

MAN.

God crowned His work of creation by making man, a personality consisting of body and soul, destined not only for the world of sensuous experience, but also for a higher moral and spiritual kingdom. Made in likeness to God, man is fitted for fellowship with Him. The unity of the human race, which is a necessary presupposition of a common redemption, lies not only in the essential similarity of the nature of all human beings, but also in their common descent from the first man.

The doctrine of man is anthropology. Theology discusses man as the subject of God's communion and redemption. Its anthropology has to do with the religious conception and destiny of man.

Man is a specially created being. He did not spring from the ground as an autochthon, as the ancients supposed, nor was he evolved from lower forms of animal life, as some modern science teaches. In the double account of his creation in Genesis a distinction is made between the creation of other animated beings and man. God made Him with special design in His own image, Gen 1:26, and by special creative activity, through which man received his life immediately from God, Gen. 2:7. He is the object of God's communion upon earth.

The biblical phrase "image of God" signifies a permanent endowment as a rational and free being, a personality, destined for moral and spiritual relations with God, Gen 1:27; 5:1; 9:6; 1 Co 11:7; Ja 3:9. The same truth is implied in the statement that God breathed into his nostrils the breath of life, Gen 2:7. The special use of the phrase, image of God, to denote the spiritual state of man, will be noted later.

The constituent parts of man are body and soul. In Genesis man is conceived in the unity of his nature rather than in the parts of his constitution. He is a living soul, that is, life embodied, an animated being, but yet the result of the union of two elements, that which is of the dust of the ground and that which was produced by the breath of the

Almighty. The unity of man's nature is of importance for the doctrines of sin and salvation; for these pertain not to a part, but to the whole of man's being.

The distinction of body and soul characterizes the entire teaching of the Bible. The Old Testament has no distinctive name for body like the New Testament. Sometimes figurative expressions are used, as "the house of clay," Job 4:19; "the sheath," Dan 7:15. The usual Old Testament name for the corporeal part of man is flesh. But the scriptural word flesh, both in the Old and New Testament, connotes more than the body. It denotes the whole man, but on his creaturely side as finite and earthly, with the concomitant idea of frailty and dependence, in contrast with spirit, which as the power of life comes directly from God. Hence the scriptural antithesis between flesh and spirit is by no means equivalent to the difference of body and soul. The body is the material organism, which does not exist for itself, but as the organ of the soul, adapted to its life. The scriptural view of the body as an integral part of man is as far removed from the false spiritualizing, which regards the body as a prison and restraint of the soul, as from materialism, which identifies the whole of human life with the life of the body.

For the incorporeal part of man Scripture uses two terms: spirit and soul. These terms are often interchangeable, but not synonymous. Spirit is the principle of life, or life itself as bestowed by the Creator; soul denotes life as constituted in nature. It is the difference of animating principle and animated result. The soul is not a third something between spirit and body, but spirit as it lives in the body.

The distinction between spirit and soul in the Bible gives ground for the question as to the dichotomy (consisting of two parts) or trichotomy (consisting of three parts) of man's constitution. Sometimes spirit and soul are spoken of as if they were distinct entities, 1 Th 5:23; Heb 4:12. But in such cases soul and spirit do not signify separate substances, nor even faculties, but different aspects of the one inner life. The bipartite division is the biblical view. Cf. Ps 63:1; Job 14:22; Mt 10:28; 2 Co 4:16. Christian theologians have differed on this point in all ages. Among the Greek fathers the tripartite view prevailed until it received a severe shock in the Apollinarian controversy. Latin and scholastic theology favored the bipartite view, as did also Luther (though not without some tripartite utterances) and the old Lutheran dogmaticians. In modern times both views have found advocates.

The importance of the idea of the unity of the human race has been referred to. It is implied in the scriptural account of the creation of man, and in St. Paul's declaration that "through one man sin entered into the world," Ro 5:12. It is also implied in the contrast between Adam and Christ, as heads of the race, 1 Co 15:22. It is distinctly stated in Act 17:26 : "He made of one every nation of men." The considerations involved in this unity have been so well summarized by Hase, that we here translate his language:

> "The descent of all men from one pair is probable according to the natural law of parsimony, confirmed by the fruitfulness of the union of persons of the most diverse color and physique, not contradicted by the difference of races with the principal organs in common and with many intermediate gradations, compatible with dispersion in all parts of the earth by emigration and natural revolutions, significant for the

recognition of the equality and brotherhood of all men, and dogmatically important for the conception of original sin."

The relation of the individual to the race gives interest to the question of the origin of the individual soul. The principal theories on this subject are preexistentianism, creationism and traducianism. The theory that souls preexist in another world and enter into earthly bodies, came into Jewish (Wisdom 8:20) and Christian circles from Greek philosophy. Among modern theologians it was adopted by Julius Muller. It has absolutely no foundation in Scripture and conflicts with the unity of the human race. The doctrine of the separate creation of every soul, while bodies are derived by heredity, was taught by many of the Church Fathers and is the prevailing view among Roman Catholic and Reformed theologians. It has apparent support in the Bible, Is 57:16; Jer 38:16. But such passages do not teach the separate creation of the soul. They refer to the general creative work of God, of which souls are the example. Traducianism, the theory that the soul is propagated with the body, is the teaching of Gregory of Nyssa and Tertullian among the Church Fathers, and of Luther and Lutheran theologians generally. While it would be too much to claim it as a doctrine of the Bible, nevertheless it accords with the whole tenor of Bible doctrine. It harmonizes with the unity of the human race, with the unity of the human personality, and with the doctrine of hereditary sin. But there is one element of truth in creationism, which must be combined with the traducian view. Notwithstanding the influence of heredity, man is born not only a type of the race, but an individual, in the endowment of whose personality God is active in a creative way.

THE ORIGINAL STATE OF MAN.

Man was created to walk with God. His original state was such as to fit him for this communion. It was a state of integrity, that is, of unimpaired purity and harmony of intellect, will and feelings, and of potential immortality. The scriptural phrase "image of God" is used in a restricted sense to denote this original state. The moral and spiritual purity of man in his primitive state is called original righteousness, and this was natural and created.

The interest of theology in the original state of man is not merely historical. The view taken of man's primitive condition and powers is of decisive importance for the view of what redemption brings to man. In general it may be claimed that high views of man's primitive state require high views of what Christ did for man. For as one thinks of Adam, so he thinks of the fall, and as he thinks of the fall, so he thinks of Christ's remedial work.

The theological term, integrity, is used in its original Latin sense to denote what is unimpaired. Applied to man's original state, it expresses the idea of physical, intellectual and spiritual soundness, wholeness and perfection. As created by God, Adam was in every sense good.

Image of God is the phrase that describes the original dignity of man. Scholasticism and Roman and Greek Catholic theology distinguish between the image of God, which denotes the natural element in the divine correspondence, and the similitude of God, which denotes the higher spiritual element. This is an artificial distinction. For image and similitude are synonyms. But the phrase image of God is used in theology with a twofold application, for which there is a basis in biblical usage. It denotes, on the one hand, what is essential to the nature of man as a personality. And as man remains a personality after the fall, the image of God in this sense was not lost in the fall, Gen 5:3; 1 Co 11:7; Ja 3:9. On the other hand, it is restricted to the moral and religious nature, and in this application it denotes the holy and immortal quality which is recovered through Christ, Col 3:10; Eph 4:24. This is the image of God which was lost in the fall.

The original Man was created in perfection, but with a described development before him. We cannot ascribe all the developed perfection, to which saints are brought in Christ, to him in his original state. The account of Adam in Eden represents man in unobstructed communion with God and with a correct knowledge of God, but without a knowledge of good and evil, which comes by experience. But he was good, and by his communion with God he was set upon the way to attain the highest spiritual possibilities and the realization of immortality. His goodness was the goodness of endowment and not yet that of attainment by self-determination; for he could fall. The state of Adam is not inaptly called by Luther in his Commentary on Genesis "puerile innocence" in contrast with the "perfect innocence," which belongs to the future spiritual life in glory. However, it was not merely a state of negative innocence, a neutral state, neither good nor bad. Adam was in an absolutely normal state, that is, positively good, a state of unimpaired purity and harmony of all his powers of body and soul. There may be room for a difference of opinion as to how far his goodness was potential or actual righteousness; but in view of the mode of his creation and of the association with God, which he had from the first awakening into life, it must be maintained that it was not necessary to pass through a development in order to attain to the state and quality of righteousness. His development would normally have been a progress in goodness, not unto good ness.

Immortality was the correlate of man's freedom from sin. For sin and death are correlates just as righteousness and life are. But as man's moral state could change, so immortality could give place to mortality. Augustine has given pointed formulation to the ideas here involved. The original state was an ability not to sin and die. By adhering to goodness this would have become an inability to sin and die. But by the fall into sin it became an inability not to sin and die.

Original righteousness belonged to the first man as he rose to life under the breath of God. That is to say it was co-created with him. There is an important difference here between Protestant and Roman Catholic theology, which has vital consequences in the conception of original sin, redemption and justification. Roman Catholic theology views original righteousness not as concreated, but as a supernatural element added to man's natural constitution. It is a superadded gift. This view introduces a dualism of nature and grace into the original condition of man. It implies that by nature man had power to do good, but that he lacked spiritual equilibrium, and needed an added endowment of grace to prevent an inner moral contradiction. In opposition to this conception Protestantism correctly asserts that from the beginning man was a harmonious unity. His state of nature was as such a state of grace. He needed no supernatural gift to preserve his spiritual balance. He was created not only for, but in communion with God.

CHAPTER III
SIN
THE COMMUNION OF MAN WITH GOD DISTURBED BY SIN

THE STATE OF CORRUPTION

Man, created in communion with God, is no longer by nature in that communion. His present spiritual condition is one of sinful corruption. Both the Scriptures and experience teach that sin is universal, and that the root of moral evil is inherent in the present nature of man.

No problem of human life has been the subject of more earnest thought in all ages and lands than the existence of moral evil. Mankind has ever been perplexed about its origin as well as its cure. The universality of sin is recognized everywhere. Universal experience teaches it. Numerous expressions of the grave fact emerge in the history and discourses contained in the Bible. But the Scriptures testify not only to the universality of sin, but also to its inherence in the nature of man. The most ancient history confirms it, as Gen 8:21; the prophets also, as Is 48:8; likewise the Psalms, as 51:5; 58:3; 143:2; and other poetical books, as Job 4:18; Eccl 7:20; Jesus most solemnly, as Jn 3:6; and in extended argument St. Paul, Ro 1-3.

This universal morally evil state is not merely a nature condition of retarded development, nor a natural imperfection, nor even a mere disease. It is nothing less than a corruption, in the true sense of that word; an impairment of the original nature of man, a vitiation of the springs of his thoughts, desires and actions. Man is no longer morally as he was created, and his nature is no longer as it was designed by his Maker. The Scriptures teach emphatically that the state of corruption was not original. Philosophy and science, unable to account for the presence of moral evil, have in one way and another conceived it as original with man. But Christianity with its moral conception of the holiness of God and of the dignity of man, tolerates no such thought. It rejects an evolution in the moral nature of man, according to which the human race is gradually emerging from an inheritance of moral evil from animal ancestors. It rejects that philosophical doctrine of evolution which makes the existence of moral evil a necessary step in human progress, which, in other words, predicates a fall that was a fall forward, instead of a descent to a lower level of life and an alienation from God. The present sinful state in no way has its roots in the created nature of man.

THE FALL

The universality of sin presupposes a crisis in the beginning of the history of man, such as the Bible describes in the fall of Adam, by which the spiritual nature of man was corrupted and his fellow ship with God was broken.

Here we have to do with a historical fact. The record of this fact is in the third chapter of Genesis. Literary and historical criticism has often been at work to dissolve the fact preserved in that record. Is the story allegory, myth or history? The allegorical view was maintained by the Alexandrian Jews (Philo) and passed over into the Alexandrian school of Christian theology (Clement, Origen). But the allegorical method of dealing with Scripture has long been discredited. The writer of that narrative was evidently not drawing a symbolical picture, but was writing down what he conceived to be an actual event. Modern criticism generally operates with the idea of myth. According to this view the narrator wrote what he conceived to be history, but what was in fact only a clothing of prevailing religious ideas in the form of a story. This view cannot be admitted. Among those who hold to the historical character of the record, there is a difference of opinion as to the literal acceptance of all the details. There is nothing intrinsically impossible in the narrative, and the artless, child-like conditions described correspond well with the infancy of the race. But what is more significant is the fact that the event of the fall, both as a historical presupposition and in its consequences, is interwoven with the whole doctrine of redemption taught throughout the Bible. Explaining away the story of the fall is not only a manipulation of Genesis, but a tampering with vital parts of the New Testament based upon it.

There is indeed a remarkable absence of allusion in other places of to the narrative of the fall in the Old Testament, scripture Job 31:33 and Hosea 6:7 possibly look back to the transgression of Adam, but as "Adam" is a general word for man, it is doubtful. But in the New Testament allusions to the narrative in Genesis are frequent and for the most part of fundamental importance for the truth of redemption. Cf. Jn 8 :44 ; Ro 5:12, 6:23; 1 Co 15:22; 2 Co 11:3; 1 Tim 2:14; 1 Jn 3:8; Rev 12:9.

The essential fact in the fall is the disobedience of Adam towards God's commandment, Ro 5:19. That act of disobedience signalized a change in the relation of man's soul to God. The harmony with God is broken. The sense of fear and shame on the part of man after the deed, which made the man and his wife hide themselves from the presence of

Jehovah, and the curse pronounced by God give evidence of the magnitude of the breach that had occurred and that must last until God has restored peace and communion through the seed of the woman.

In the conception of the narrator of the scriptural story of the fall there was undoubtedly something about "The tree of the knowledge of good and evil," which brought both knowledge and death. Was that merely a childish superstition? We cannot believe it. But certainly the fruit of the tree did not cause death as a poison nor knowledge by physical effect. The tree was more than symbol; it was instrument. Death and the knowledge of good and evil came to man by his disobedience of God's commandment, but that disobedience was exercised in reference to the tree which God had singled out. There was an instrumental significance about the tree, but the moral nature of man was not corrupted physically by the fruit, but by the transgression manifested in the eating.

It is not stated in Genesis that there was an unseen power working through the serpent for the fall of man, but this is implied, and in Rev 12:9; 20:2 the serpent is distinctly called Satan. Our Lord's utterance that characterizes the devil as a murderer from the beginning, Jn 8:44, may perhaps directly refer to the murder of Abel; but it proves that He conceived moral evil to be caused by the devil from the beginning. St. Paul applies the language of the curse upon the serpent to Satan, Ro 16:20. The curse and promise in Gen 3:15 distinctly imply that there was an invisible power of evil at work in the serpent, for the enmity predicted between the two "seeds" is manifestly not an enmity between man and snakes, but between those who under the grace of God clung to Him and those who under the power of the Wicked One chose evil for their good, as the subsequent story in Genesis illustrates in the lines of the Sethites and Cainites. In that feature of the story of the fall, which accounts for sin by the seduction of the Serpent and the disobedience of man, this important doctrinal truth is emphatically brought out: that sin came by the will of man, and that God is in no sense the cause of sin. So the Bible teaches everywhere, Ps 5:4; 1 Jn 1:5; Ja 1:13.

THE ESSENCE OF SIN

Sin is essentially disobedience to God, and it involves the sinner in guilt and the liability to punishment.

The inner connection between the three ideas of sin, guilt and punishment must be observed. Disobedience to God would be of no moral consequence unless it involved the sinner in guilt. And guilt would not be manifested unless God reacted against it in punishment. So the inevitable consequences of sin are guilt and punishment. Conscience makes a man feel his guilt more or less keenly. But guilt must not be identified with the consciousness of it; for it is not a subjective feeling, but an objective relation to God. What God has against anyone, that is his guilt. In legal terms guilt is the measure of unsatisfied responsibility to the law. Corresponding to the guilt of man is the reaction of God's holiness against it, what the Scriptures denominate the wrath of God, which is not an emotion like human anger, but nevertheless a real reaction of God condemning guilt. It manifests itself as punishment. Therefore sin brings man into guilt and exposes Him to the wrath of God and punishment.

The vocabulary of Scripture is rich in terms for sin. But the Bible contains no definition of sin. The statement in

1 Jn 3:4, "Sin is lawlessness," is not a definition, but a characterization of one vital aspect of sin. The Bible speaks of specific acts of sin, although in the New Testament the idea of sin as a principle working in man is made prominent. The chief terms in the Old Testament are "*chattath*" and "*pesha.*" The former is from the idea of missing the mark, and hence implies lack of conformity to a standard. The latter is translated transgression, but contains the idea of rebellion and implies an offense against a person or authority. This is the deeper and more predominant idea of sin in both the Old Testament and the New. In the New Testament the general word is "*hamartia*," which etymologically expresses the mild idea of missing the mark, but in its use both for acts of sin and the principle of sin expresses the gravest offence against God. The terms "*parabasis*" and "*paraptoma*" imply a lack of conformity to the standard of the law. But "*asebeia*" is disregard of God's person, ungodliness. It expresses the dominant biblical thought of sin as offence and rebellion against the person of God.

When conscience becomes awake to sin, even if it be a wrong done to man, it always sees God. This is in accord with the scriptural teaching that all sin is an offence against God. Cf. Gen 39:9; Ps 51:4.

Luther made unbelief the root of all sins, and in this he was followed by Lutheran theology. If, however, we inquire further into the motive principle of unbelief in man, we must find it in selfishness. Sin is the attempt or desire to attain some imagined good or satisfaction apart from God. It places self instead of God at the center of one's life. The tracing of all sins back to one root like unbelief or selfishness guards from atomistic conceptions of sin. By atomistic is meant a conception which sees sins only singly and quantitatively. Such a view looks only upon the surface. It does not penetrate to the principle of sin. But man has not only sins, but sin.

Sin is personal, voluntary. Only a moral being can sin. The seat of sin is in the center of the moral personal life, the will. Thence it permeates the whole being of man. A man cannot be sinful in part and pure in part, sinful in body and pure in mind. The false idea often prevails, and it has been erroneously attributed to biblical writers, that sin has its source and seat in the sensuous or bodily part of man. Closely akin to this false notion is the other error that sin grows out of the finiteness of man. Beneath both of these conceptions there lurks the thought that the Creator is really the author of sin by the natural constitution, which He gave to man. Moreover, in this way sin is shifted from a moral to a physical basis. Sin is not simply a backward stage of nature, out of which man may ultimately come by development and increasing power of mind over the body; nor is it merely a fault in respect to what man has not yet attained. As man was created by God, there was no natural basis for the conflict of sin in him. Sin is seated in the will of man.

Although sin is fundamentally in the will of man, it is not necessarily a conscious, deliberate transgression of a known command. A corrupt state of the will, underlying deliberate choices and acts, is also sin. In the New Testament the word sin often designates a state in sin, and when man is said to be flesh, in the peculiar religious and ethical sense in which the term is often used, it is with the connotation that sin is inherent in man. "Thou must not understand 'flesh,' therefore, as though that only were flesh which is connected with unchastity, but St. Paul uses 'flesh' of the whole man, body and soul, reason and all his faculties included, because all that is in him longs and strives after the flesh." This description of "flesh" from Luther's Preface to the Epistle to the Romans is quoted approvingly in Thayer's Lexicon of the New Testament.

ORIGINAL SIN

The fall of Adam left him in a permanently sinful state, which by heredity also passed over to his descendants. This hereditary sinful condition of man is called original sin. Its elements are, on the negative side, the absence of original righteousness, on the positive side, concupiscence, which is sin.

A misapprehension, suggested by the word meaning "original", must here be guarded against. Original sin, as the phrase is used in theology, does not denote Adam's transgression, but our sin by nature and inheritance. The word original in this connection means pertaining to origin, and is applied to sin in reference to our parental origin and descent. The term comes from Tertullian.

The doctrine of original sin, as it has been developed in the Church, has grown out of the theology of St. Paul, as it has been formulated especially in the epistle to the Romans. But the doctrine has support in all parts of the Bible. In the Old Testament three facts, essential to the doctrine, stand out prominently: the universality of sin, the hereditary character of sin, and the solidarity of the human race. But it should be remarked that these facts are nowhere explicitly connected with Adam. These three facts are also presupposed everywhere in the New Testament, and in two places they are explicitly connected with Adam, Ro 5:12; 1 Co 15:22. That the universality of sin is everywhere presupposed in the Bible has already been shown. It has also been shown that the hereditary character of sin and its natural inherence are general scriptural teachings, Gen 6:3; 8:21; Ps 51:5; 58:3; Job 14:4; 25:4; Mt 15:19; Jn 3:6. The solidarity or moral unity of the human race is a conception which pervades the whole of Scripture. From the non-scientific character of the biblical writings it is not to be expected that there should be formal statements of the doctrine. But it appears in the Old Testament in the way the individual always regarded himself as a part of some collective whole. For instance, he realized his relation to God, not as standing alone, but as part of the covenant people. This, it is true, applies only to Israel. But the relation of nations expressed in the genealogical tables in Genesis gives the conception of solidarity world-wide significance. In the New Testament the solidarity of mankind lies in the idea of the "world" as the object of God's saving love in Christ. It has a natural basis in the unity of the race.

It is on the basis of these three fundamental truths, the universality and heredity of sin and the solidarity of mankind, that St. Paul makes the sin, which is the cause of universal death, the sin of Adam. In Ro 5:12 the apostle (as Bengel correctly remarks) is not expressly speaking of "original sin", but of sin generically or as a principle. But he plainly indicates that this evil principle, whose universality is evidenced by the universality of death, is to be traced back to Adam. Cf. also 1 Co 15:22. Conceiving of mankind as a moral unity, he can say that all sinned when through one man sin entered into the world. But this is not to be understood in the legally constructive sense, afterwards used by theologians in their theories of original sin, that the will of Adam was the will of all men, or that the trespass of Adam (his individual act as distinguished from the principle of sin) is legally

imputed to every individual as his deed and the ground of his
condemnation. The judgment came unto all men to
condemnation through one trespass (v. 18) because that
trespass was the entering in of the death-bearing principle of
sin. Through the principle of sin, fundamentally and primarily
manifested in mankind in Adam, all were made sinners. At
any stage the race may be considered as a unity in sin, and St.
Paul goes back to the initial state in Adam. But the moral
unity implies a natural unity. As all participate in Adam's
nature, so all participate in the principle of sin which was
manifested in his trespass. St. Paul does not expressly say, but
obviously implies that all share by heredity in the principle of
sin which was in Adam. Not only Adam's sinful nature, but
also Adam's sin was inherited. Through the one man's
disobedience the many were made sinners (v. 19), not by
legally construing his individual act as their deed, but by his
sin as a hereditary evil principle passing unto all. As death
passed unto all men, so sin passed unto all by heredity, its
presence being proved by the universality of death. The
underlying thought of St. Paul is not that of an abstract legal
liability of one person for the deed of another, but the
realistic conception of the solidarity of mankind found in the
Old Testament. Adam was the race; the race is Adam
extended and unfolded. There is an analogy to this in the way
individual names in the Old Testament stand for the whole
tribe or nation. This unfolding of the race is by natural
descent, and with the propagation of Adam there is a
propagation of his sin. The contrasted conception in St. Paul,
of the imputation of Christ's righteousness, is also based
upon the idea of racial unity in Him as the second Adam. But
here the unity is spiritual, for the last Adam became a life-

giving spirit. That which is natural is first, then that which is spiritual. Cf. 1 Co 15:45.

This fact of universal human sinfulness, inseparable from the natural and moral connection with Adam's sin, is what is meant by original sin. Negatively, it is the absence of original righteousness, that is, of the spiritual and moral quality which should belong to man according to God's creation. Man is not born in the communion of God, as Adam was created, but, like fallen Adam, in alienation from God. He stands in need of redemption to restore him to the true fear, trust and love of God. Since original righteousness is also called the image of God, original sin on the negative side has been correctly denned as the privation of the image of God.

Positively, original sin is concupiscence, that is, evil inclination, coveting, which includes not only sensual desires, but also all desires against the will of God. The loss of original righteousness has not left man in a state of moral indifference. Not being good, he is bad. Where holiness and righteousness should exist, there is a positive depravation of man's nature, a corrupt state which is the source of evil desires and thoughts. So Jesus said: "Out of the heart come forth evil thoughts," Mt 15:19. By this indwelling concupiscence man is in bondage to the law of sin, Ro 7:7sq. The higher powers of mind and will are vitiated no less than the sensual nature of man. Concupiscence as such is sin ; it is not merely what is called in Roman Catholic theology "*fomes peccati*", the kindling material for sin. The Scriptures connote man's subjection to concupiscence by the term flesh, used in its peculiar ethical sense. Man is flesh when he is not governed by the Spirit of God. "The mind of the flesh is enmity against God," Ro 8:7. So it is opposed to spirit, Jn 3:6.

Three characteristics of original sin are theologically important: its heredity (generatedness) , its natural inherence, and its ineradicability. Original sin is inseparable from natural generation. Christ in His sinlessness is not an exception to this, because He was not naturally generated, but miraculously conceived. Roman Catholics make an exception of the mother of Christ and claim that she was immaculately conceived. This is an unfounded assumption necessary for their Mariolatry. Original sin is inherent, but not integral in the present nature of man. A gifted Lutheran theologian of the sixteenth century, Mathias Flacius, fell into the error of making original sin of the substance of man. Lutheran theology discarded this teaching. The first section of the Formula of Concord is directed against it. But the Lutheran Church confessionally and correctly insists that original sin inheres in man's nature so completely as to corrupt it through and through. This is known as the doctrine of total depravity. Original sin is never eradicated from man in this life. Baptism removes the guilt of original sin, but sinful concupiscence remains until the redeemed of Christ pass from a state of grace to a state of glory.

The Augsburg Confession, Art. II, says : "Original sin is truly sin, condemning and bringing eternal death." In the explication of this doctrine some scholastic theologians of the seventeenth century distinguished a twofold imputation of Adam's sin to man for condemnation, mediate and immediate. By mediate imputation is meant that the sin of Adam is accounted man's unrighteousness inasmuch as that sin is mediated or transmitted through inherited and inherent depravity. By immediate imputation is meant that we are accounted guilty before God, apart from our own personal sinfulness, on account of the transgression of Adam, since he was the representative of the race and his deed of transgression was the deed of all. The doctrine of mediate imputation is undoubtedly in harmony with the scriptural ideas of heredity and solidarity. But the theory of an immediate imputation of Adam's transgression as such is an unsuccessful attempt to define further the biblical conception of our participation in Adam's sin by an artificial legal construction. Adam did not act as the legal representative of his descendants. That idea cannot be found in the Bible. His sin was their sin because at that stage he was the race. The underlying idea is that of the real unity of the human race, which is moral as well as physical. But Adam's transgression is not to be logically separated from his sin, which continues to manifest itself in his descendants in what is called the old Adam, as a separate element in what is imputed as original sin. This abstract theory of an immediate legal imputation of Adam's transgression is not found in the Lutheran confessions nor in the early Lutheran theologians. Koestlin in his work on Luther's Theology declared he could find no trace of it in Luther. Eminent Lutheran theologians of recent times reject it, as it is rejected here. Early Lutheran theology laid all stress upon the actual inherent depravity of human nature inherited from Adam. Incidentally it may be remarked that Calvin did the same.

FORMS OF SIN

The inherent sinfulness, which is common to all men, is manifested in individual life in a great variety of developments and forms, so that different classes of sins may be distinguished as well as different stages in sin.

Stages in the sinful life mark the progress of the development of the principle of sin in man. In the development of the individual personality there is a growth in sin, or, taking the influences of divine grace into view, an arresting or retarding of the natural growth in sin. The latter feature in the development will properly receive consideration when the operation of the grace of the Holy Spirit is discussed. In the progression of a sinful life towards a confirmed conscious and determined opposition to God it is customary to distinguish four stages: bondage, security, hypocrisy, and hardening. The state of bondage is the universal condition of servitude to sin, the common form of sinful corruption without distinctive features of individual development in sin, Jn 8:34; Ro 6:16. The state of security is the condition of one who yields to his sinful desires without serious thought, scruple of conscience or restraint from within. It is that form of carnal life in which evil desire is permitted to reign without resistance. Conscience makes it impossible for any man to be absolutely in a state of security in regard to his sin. The state of hypocrisy is characterized by a conscious, deliberate choice of sin against better knowledge and profession. It is attended by specious self-justification and argumentation to give a righteous appearance to one's acts. The state of hardening is the condition in which the heart has become impervious to the truth and inaccessible to the grace of God. In the Scriptures this state is represented as a judgment of God, who righteously punishes sin with sin. Cf. Ex 4:21; Is 6:9; Mt 13:14; Ro 1:24; 2 Co 3:14.

Classifications of sin indicate the modes in which the principle of sin is manifested. Prior to all classifications is the fundamental distinction between habitual and actual sin. Habitual sin is the same as original sin, so called with reference to the condition (habitus) of man. Actual sins are either internal motions of desire and will or external acts. There are numerous classifications of these. For practical uses a table of classification is inserted here. Sins may be classified with respect to:

1. The object: against God, a neighbor, one's self.
2. The law: commission or omission.
3. The sphere of the act: internal and external; or, of the heart, the tongue, the hand.
4. The person sinning: our own sins, and those of others in which we participate.
5. The intention: voluntary and involuntary. The latter subdivided into sins of ignorance, precipitancy and infirmity.
6. The effect: mute and crying. For the latter term cf. Gen 4:10; Ja 5:4.
7. The circumstances: lighter and more grievous.
8. The guilt, venial and mortal.

For the latter term cf. 1 Jn 5:16. Venial sins are not without guilt, but as they are venial and not attended with a loss of faith, they are at once forgiven for Christ's sake. Mortal sins are not simply gross vices, such as medieval writers included in lists like the seven mortal sins, nor certain categories of sins such as the Roman Catholic Church pronounces mortal in contrast with venial or trivial sins. Mortal sins are sins attended with a loss of faith. In the case of the unbeliever there can be no venial sins, because he does not live in the daily forgiveness of sins for Christ's sake. The sin against the Holy Spirit is distinguished from other mortal sins, which admit of repentance and forgiveness. The sin against the Holy Spirit, which Christ describes in Mt 12:31;

Lu 12:10, is that persevering resistance to the grace of God, which precludes repentance and faith and therefore the conditions upon which forgiveness can be received.

BONDAGE OF THE WILL

After the fall of man sin became a fixed hereditary condition of depravity, which involves an inability truly to fear, love and trust in God. This natural depravity affects all the powers of man, but since these powers center morally in the will, it has become customary to speak of the bondage of the will.

In dealing with this difficult but important subject it is necessary to have a clear idea of what is involved in the conception of the bondage of the will and the related conception of total depravity. When a recent author, referring to this doctrine as it is stated in a Calvinistic confession, declares that Jesus "did not represent all men as being as bad as they can be and that from the very moment of birth," we encounter such a misunderstanding. It is not meant that men are as bad as they can be. The devils are as bad as they can be; but men are not born devils. They are redeemable. Nor is it the meaning that the faculties of the human mind have been destroyed, that man has no real, but only a seeming will. By the fall he has not ceased to be a man, a moral personality, having all the faculties which belong to the constitution of humanity. When it is asserted that sin corrupts man's nature, that it pervades all his faculties, it is not denied that the faculties are still there. Misunderstanding also may arise from the mention of the will only in the phrase, bondage of the will. The question is, as Chemnitz clearly stated, concerning the powers of man. What spiritual powers remain to him in his sinful state? For the darkened understanding and the perverted affections are as much a part of this bondage as the obliquity of the will. The test must be made not on the lower plane of man's actions, his social, domestic and civil relations when these are considered apart from the relation to God, but on the highest plane. In his relations to God, and in his relation to men and things as these reflect his relations to God, can man by nature be right and get right by himself? If he can, then the doctrine of the bondage of the will is an error; but if he cannot, then the enthralling power of indwelling sin is established. As the matter is to be viewed in these highest relations, the question takes the form: What spiritual powers remain to man after the fall? Melanchthon, in the Augsburg Confession and in the Apology, wisely fixed the question at this point: Can man truly fear, love and trust in God?

There have been variations of opinion on this question in all ages of the Church. Rarely have theologians dared to maintain equality of man's powers before and after the fall. But the extent of the loss of spiritual powers has been variously conceived. But before the history of the variant views is sketched, it is necessary to examine the teaching of the Scriptures. Here we note first the general fact that the doctrine of redemption has for its presupposition the helplessness of man in sin. Taking up the Old Testament we observe the demand of a renewal of the heart before there can be peace with God. This demand for renewal by God implies the powerlessness expressed by the phrase, bondage of the will. Cf. Ps 51:10 ; Jer 24:7, Ez 11:19. The teaching of Jesus begins with a call to repentance, implying that the mind and will of men are depraved, Mt 4:17; Lu 24:47. It addresses itself to the sick who need a physician, Mt 9:12 ; Mk 2:17 ; Lu

5:31; to the lost who need to be sought and found, Lu 15:3. He declares men to be servants of sin, who need to be set free, Jn 8:34; and to be flesh, who are not fit for the kingdom of God, Jn 3:6. St. Peter and St. James teach the necessity of regeneration, implying inability to fulfill the righteousness of God, 1 P 1:23; Ja 1:18. St. Paul is especially explicit. The natural man is the old man, who needs to be made a new man, Ro 6 :4-6 ; Eph 4:22-24; Col 3:9. The natural man is the servant of sin, Ro 6:16, 17; carnal, sold under sin, Ro 7:14. St. Paul is very severe in describing the flesh-mind, Ro 8:5. Cf. Eph 2:3. The natural is the contrary of the spiritual, receiving not the things of the Spirit of God, 1 Co 2:14. It is not a contradiction of the spiritual powerlessness of man, when the Scriptures recognize natural affection and virtues. Jesus declares that men know how to give good gifts to their children, yet he says they are evil, Mt 7:11. St. Paul describes it as an extreme of depravity when among other faults they are without natural affection, 2 Tim 3:3. He recognizes that the "unbeliever" may have the virtue of providing for his own household, 1 Tim 5:8. Natural virtue is not yet spiritual goodness, nor is the man who has it free from the taint of sin in mind and heart.

According to these scriptural testimonies, what is called the bondage of the will signifies that man has lost the center of gravity in his spiritual and moral life. That center is no longer in God, where it should be. The man remains, but by nature he is now, so to speak, spiritually eccentric. The natural faculties of thinking, willing and feeling were not destroyed by sin, but have received a moral and spiritual twist. The exercise of these powers for true spiritual ends is no longer subject to the will of God. Communion with God is broken. The mind of man is darkened, the desires are unregulated, and the will is impotent to assume a true God-ward direction. Man cannot begin or maintain communion with God through his own sin-permeated powers. All that remains to him is the possibility of being redeemed and restored to fellowship with God through divine grace. The darkening and impotency of the mind and will are not such as to obliterate conscience, moral action and a natural knowledge of God. But whatever man chooses as good, he no longer chooses it from pure love to God, nor can he. All is tainted by sin.

The distinction between the powers that were lost by sin and the powers that remain is drawn in the Lutheran confessions in these terms: man has power in *civilibus*, but not in *spiritualibus*. As between man and man, there is right and wrong moral conduct among men, apart from regeneration to a Christian life. But as between man and God, man in his sin cannot establish right spiritual relations. These are effected by God alone through grace. Spiritual deeds imply the possession of the Holy Spirit, and the natural is not in the communion of the Holy Spirit.

This doctrine of the spiritual incapacity of the natural man has had a checkered history in the Church. The early Christian teachers after the apostles, especially the Greek fathers, desiring to oppose the fatalism of philosophy, emphasized the freedom of the will, while teaching a power of sin that made redemption necessary. The Latin fathers had a deeper appreciation of the inherent corruption of man. The controversy between Augustine and Pelagius at the beginning of the fifth century brought into sharp antithesis the implications of the bondage of sin on the one side, and of freedom of the will on the other. Pelagius regarded the will as essentiallly unimpaired by the fall. Magnifying the power of man, he minimized the effects of the fall and also of redemption. Augustine felt that the powerlessness of the will for good could scarcely be overstated, and magnified the grace of God. Semipelagianism in the same age regarded the powers of man as injured, but not rendered entirely ineffectual. It perpetuated Eastern views in the West. The Augustinian view, somewhat moderated, passed over to the Church of the Middle Ages, but Semipelagian views penetrated into scholastic theology more and more and prevail in the Roman Catholic Church to this day. The Reformation returned to the Augustinian teaching, at first in an extreme form. The teaching of salvation by grace alone through faith made necessary the emphasizing of the bondage of the will. Luther defended his doctrine against Erasmus in his book *De Servo Arbitrio*. A modified Semipelagianism, called synergism, again crept into the Lutheran Church under the influence of Melanchthon and became one of the causes for the writing of the Formula of Concord. Early in the seventeenth century reaction against Calvinism, which, with absolute predestination, taught the bondage of the will, produced Arminianism with its strong assertion of the freedom and power of the human will. Modern theology is generally characterized by a critical attitude towards the doctrine of the bondage of the will and an inclination to recognize a sinful bias rather than a dominion of sin in man.

THE ATTITUDE OF GOD TOWARD SIN.

Sin being present in the world contrary to the will of God, He directs the history of the world so as to overcome it. In His holiness He reacts against it in judgment, but at the same time reveals His gracious purpose to save the world from it.

God's attitude towards sin is historically revealed in His dealings with men and nations. This historically applies to all history, but in a special way His attitude is made known through the history recorded in the Scriptures. It should be observed that God's attitude towards sin is revealed not only in that form of the divine Word which is called the Law and which presents commandments and threats of judgment. It is also exhibited in that other form of divine Word which is called the Gospel and which presents God's promises and provision of salvation from sin.

God hates sin. However human the word hate may sound, it is the right word. As a personal Being of perfect moral purity, God hates sin. In the majesty of His nature He sets Himself against it. The word which expresses the inviolable dignity of the divine nature is holiness. Holiness is more than goodness. It includes goodness and every other attribute of divinity, for holiness is the quality of divinity itself. So the word is used in the Bible. Sin is an encroachment upon the divinity of God. Therefore with His whole nature, that is, in His holiness, God reacts against sin and antagonizes it without compromise or cessation. In His holiness God reacts against sin to condemn it. It is hostile reaction. It manifests itself in judgments. It displays itself as divine anger. When the Scriptures speak so frequently of the wrath of God which is revealed against all unrighteousness of men, it is not a mere anthropomorphism, nor does it express love seen from the reverse side. Certainly God's anger is not a fitful, unreasoning passion, like much human anger. The wrath of God is a positive displeasure, displaying itself in real energetic reaction and in painful and destructive effects. In

His wrath God sets Himself against sin as that which ought not to exist.

God's holiness expresses itself in the form of punishments upon sinners. He brings judgments upon sinners in this life for unrighteousness, and upon those who will not allow themselves to be separated from sin He has threatened to inflict punishments in the life to come. It is not necessary to adduce specific instances of these scriptural truths; but it is necessary to remember, what is often forgotten, that the evils which men suffer as hindrances in the development of their lives, and especially the breakdown of death and all that leads to it, are connected with sin. Many of these evils are evidences of God's retributive justice, that is, they are punishments for sin. And even those evils which are not punishments, but disciplinary chastenings, are still connected with sin. So they also are evidence of God's reaction against sin. For the perfect have no need of disciplinary chastening.

The hostile attitude of God against sin should not be thought of apart from His eternal purpose which is to be fulfilled in the world. The presence of sin indeed crosses and disturbs the unfolding of that purpose, as it began to be realized in creation. But the divine purpose now takes sin into account and is a purpose of redemption from sin. In the fulfillment of this purpose both good and evil ripen unto the day of judgment. The tares and wheat shall grow together until the harvest. The true character of sin shall be worked out and revealed in all its ungodliness. In this process it is ordained in God's judgment that sin shall bring forth sin as a part of its punishment. As men "refused to have God in their knowledge, God gave them up unto a reprobate mind," Ro 1:18-28. But all development of sin in the world must be subsumed under the gracious purpose of God to overcome it. The ultimate design is to produce the knowledge of sin as the evil of life and to awaken yearning for deliverance from its misery, in order that finally grace may much more abound where sin has abounded, Ro 5:20. The divine provision for overcoming sin is the redemption from its guilt and domination through Christ, Ro 11:32; Jn3:17.

> "At the foundation of all lies an eternal and universal loving will of God in Christ, which aims at man and his salvation and which realizes itself in mankind redeemed by Christ and united with Him." (Luthardt)

CHAPTER IV
REDEMPTION

The Communion of Man with God Restored in the Redemption Through Christ

THE REDEMPTION THROUGH CHRIST

The communion of man with God, which was interrupted by the entrance of sin, is being restored by a divine redemption of mankind from sin. This redemption was conceived by God before the foundation of the world as a gracious purpose of salvation. It was objectively accomplished in the historical appearance of the Savior, Jesus Christ. It is subjectively applied to men by the Holy Spirit, who works in and from within the Church by divinely appointed means, called the means of grace.

At this point we come to the body of Christian theology proper. For Christian theology is essentially the doctrine of redemption. All that has hitherto been considered, God, creation and sin, constitutes the presupposition of the redemption through Christ.

The unfolding of the plan of redemption reveals the Trinity. In the successive dispensations of operation God is revealed as triune, each person of the Deity being especially manifested in one part of the whole great plan. The Father is especially manifested in the gracious purpose of salvation. God so loved the world that He gave His only begotten Son to redeem it and sent the Holy Spirit to sanctify. it. Before the foundation of the world mankind, lost in sin and alienated from God, was present to the divine mind, as St. Paul declares with such broad sweep of presentation in Eph 1:3-

10. A gracious purpose to save the world which He had made from sin and to bring it back to Himself by a universal plan of redemption was conceived by the eternal Father. The Son is more distinctly manifested in the execution of the purpose of salvation. The work of redemption was accomplished by the Son, who became incarnate and did and suffered what was necessary to overcome sin and its consequences and to lay the foundation for the regeneration of the world. He is the Redeemer in virtue of what He is in the world as well as of what He did in it. For in His person the union of man with God is complete. Communion between God and man was objectively restored in the divine-human Mediator, Christ. The Holy Spirit is more prominently revealed in the application of redemption of men. Fellowship with God can exist only where man inwardly participates in it. The redemption of Christ must be personally appropriated. Owing to man's sinful condition this is possible only by an application of the salvation, which is in Christ, to him through operations which come from God. Man by himself cannot work up to it. Salvation is brought down to man by the Holy Spirit, who effects the necessary internal changes in the soul of man by a method of grace divinely ordered. This method embraces the combining of those who are restored to the life in God into a body, the Church. In this body the Holy Spirit works and from it He works out into the sinful world through the instrumentalities of God's appointment, the means of grace.

According to this framework of the plan of salvation the discussion will now proceed in three sub divisions.
The Restoration of Sinful Man to Communion with God:

      A. Provided in the gracious purpose of God,

      B. Realized in the person and work of Christ,

C. Applied by the Holy Spirit in the Church through the means of grace.

CHAPTER V
THE GRACIOUS PURPOSE OF GOD
THE RESTORATION OF MAN TO COMMUNION WITH GOD
THROUGH CHRIST PROVIDED IN THE GRACIOUS PURPOSE
OF GOD

THE GRACIOUS WILL OF GOD

The redemption of the world from sin has its ultimate source in the love of God, which carries forward His design, that began to be realized in the creation of the world, as an eternal and universal purpose to save the world through Christ.

The subject now before us is God's counsel of redemption. In speaking of it, it will be necessary to make use of the biblical term predestination. It would perhaps be an advantage if this word could be avoided. Not that the word is objectionable in itself. But owing to long controversies in the Church, the word has gathered around itself disconcerting associations. Speak of predestination, and thought does not turn back to the eternal love which provides salvation, but at once imagination raises dreadful pictures of fixed destiny of bliss and woe. But here it is necessary to keep clear of such imaginings and to fix thought upon the love of God in Christ towards the world in sin. The gracious will of God is the subject of predestination, but not every phase of that subject can be considered here. There are aspects of it which cannot be understood until the realization of redemption and its application to men by the Holy Spirit have been comprehended. Here we view the saving love of God to the world generally, setting on one side for the present how that love will work out in any individual life. The old Lutheran dogmaticians were wont to make a distinction between the antecedent or universal and the consequent or special goodwill of God. We are not binding ourselves to their method of discussion, but the term antecedent may appropriately be applied to what we have in hand here, namely, the consideration of God's universal will of redemption.

At the outset let the connection of God's gracious purpose of redemption with His eternal design in creation creating the world be noted. As we know by experience of none but a sinful world, it is useless to speculate how God's design in creation would have been carried out if there had been no sin. What we must now keep in mind is that God, who created the world in love, redeems it in the same love, and through redemption fulfills His eternal purpose, the realization of which began in creation.

The fundamental ideas connected with God's gracious purpose of redemption are laid down by St. Paul in Eph 1:3-10. The leading conceptions are these. All that is effected for the salvation of the world is the outcome of a purpose and choice of God, formed before the foundation of the world. That choice is in Christ. There is a choice of God in Christ before the world was, a choice to save, not a choice of one person in preference to another. It is the choice of what has been historically manifested in Christ. This choice is according to the good pleasure of God's will, which He purposed in Christ unto a dispensation of the fullness of the times, i. e., with a view of historical fulfillment. This choice to save in God's own time by a historical process is carried out according to the purpose of Him who works all things after the counsel of His will. Whatever else is at work in the world, powers of physical energy or powers of human will, this eternal purpose of divine grace works through it all to the consummation of redemption, Ro 8:28. This is the gracious will of God.

New Testament terminology requires some attention here. For the gracious purpose of salvation the New Testament employs a great variety of designations according to different points of view. The point of view in every case is important. As expressive of the love which is revealed in Christ, it is called "grace," Eph 1:7; 2:7, and "mercy," Eph 2:4; Tit 3:5, and "kindness and love toward man," Tit 3 :4. Absolutely conceived, it is called "the will," Eph 1:5, and "the mystery of His will," Eph 1:9, and "the counsel of His will," Eph 1 :11. With reference to the freedom of God in providing salvation, it is called "the purpose," Eph 1:11; 2 Tim 1:9, and also "foreknowledge," Ro 8:29. In the Bible foreknowledge, according to the pregnant use of the word know, means more than prescience. God's foreknowledge signifies loving appropriation before the foundation of the world. With reference to the final goal of salvation, it is called "foreordination," Ro 8:29 ; Eph 1:5. It is called "election," Ro 9:11 ; 2 Pet 1:10, in reference to the objects of salvation, namely, sinners alienated from God and incapable of saving themselves. This word, election, easily suggests erroneous ideas. In Scripture election is choice, not choice between. This election does not denote a selection of certain persons to the exclusion or passing by of others. The antithesis implied is rather the condition of alienation from God. Out of this condition God elects objects to enjoy communion with Himself, whether a few or all, does not affect the meaning of election. Cf. the study of this and related words in

Cremer's Lexicon of New Testament Greek. God's election is in Christ, and is as universal as Christ's power to save.[3]

The gracious purpose of God is nowhere more simply and unmistakably declared than in Jn 3:16: "God so loved the world that He gave his only begotten Son," etc. This passage declares the electing love of God in the universality of His purpose to save.

The gracious purpose of God is best understood from the fulfillment of this purpose in Christ. The love of God, which has been historically revealed in Christ and which in Christ addresses itself to all men, tells us more truly what the eternal counsel of redemption in the mind of God is, than any amount of abstract reasoning about God's sovereignty and will. For the historical Christ is the eternal purpose of God in its realization. The whole revelation of God in Christ shows that His will of love is not a mere complacent desire that mankind may be saved, but an active, working purpose which provides a free, gracious, seriously intended, sufficient and efficacious salvation for all men, whose only limitation is the acceptance of the terms on which it is offered.

The Scriptures give us no right to imagine a secret will of God at work alongside of the will which is revealed, as if in God's revelation there were mental reservations. Apart from Christ there is no will of God, either saving or condemning, and what Christ is we know. Christ is the Savior, not of a selection, but of the world. In Christ the eternal purpose of God operates through the course of the world for historical fulfillment, and this purpose is not any more the fixing of a

---

[3] Voigt seems to be confusing the universal saving will of God with election. Most Lutheran theologians have confessed that God's saving will is universal, though his act of election is particular. For a full explanation of this approach, see volume 2 of this series.

closed circle of persons, by predetermination, in its scope than in the progress of its historical realization. God's goodwill remains open in its individual application until the work of redemption shall have been concluded.

THE HISTORICAL PREPARATION FOR THE REDEEMER.

The divine purpose of redemption began to be realized immediately after the fall of man in the form of a preparation of mankind for the coming Redeemer. This preparation was obtained by a providential education of the human race in general and by a special revelation of Himself, which was gradually limited to a chosen nation.

The coming Redeemer was promised directly after the fall in the person of that One of the woman's seed who should bruise the Serpent's head, Gen 3:15. The long historical interval between the fall of man and the appearance of Christ was a period of preparation for mankind. As the child is educated for the duties of manhood, so under divine pedagogy there was an education of the human race, which prepared it for the full revelation of redemption. The divine government was so exercised that the total incapacity of man for self-redemption and the need of divine salvation were demonstrated by experience. This is the negative side of the preparation. There was also a positive side, in that God vouchsafed anticipations of the coming redemption, and in that a chosen nation was trained by historical revelation to the end that all nations of the earth were to be blessed through it.

The negative preparation is especially manifest in the history of heathenism, but in part also in the experiences of recalcitrant Israel. As St. Paul testifies, God suffered all the nations but one to walk in their own ways, and yet not altogether without witness of Himself, Acts 14:16-17. They were permitted to turn to the powers of nature, which they worshiped instead of God, Ro 1:21. The result was the dawning of the consciousness of the need of salvation from heaven. On the other hand, they were permitted to develop to the fullest extent the natural life of man. The result of this was the preparation among the heathen of intellectual, social and material means for the furtherance of the knowledge of redemption, when once it was revealed.

The positive preparation was given in that direct self-manifestation of God which is called revelation. God taught mankind repentance and faith by direct manifestations of His mercy and wrath, and by words of promise and rebuke, in order that the world might be prepared to receive the Redeemer, even though at first He was received but by few. In the early history of the race this revelation was universal, but division soon set in and in the course of time the principle of particularism was introduced. The special supernatural manifestations of God were limited to a chosen people. Israel became the leading factor on the human side in the historical preparation of redemption, not however by what it contributed from its natural life, but by what it received from God. The revelation of God alone made Israel an exceptional people, Ro 9:4sq. Their history is a training in faith and repentance in the midst of the corruptions of sin by divinely given laws and promises.

The collection of all the laws of Israel, religious, moral and civil, is called the Law. By it the Jewish people were organized into a theocracy, a people under God's rule, among whom the ground was prepared for the manifestation of the future redemption. The Law was a spiritual means of grace, Ro 7:12. But it consisted largely of external ceremonial and civil regulations, which operated towards holiness of life and heart from without. To understand the full significance of the Old Testament Law, two aspects of it must be observed. Positively, it revealed the God of salvation and therefore was a source of delight to the devout believer in Jehovah. This is the aspect which is made more prominent in the Old Testament, as in some of the psalms. Negatively, the Law also revealed the sinfulness of man and the character of sin and so was a pedagogue to Christ. This is the aspect emphasized by St. Paul, Ro 3:20; Gal 3:24.

The promises were given in prophecy and predicted the future glory of Israel and the coming of the divine Messiah. In this Messiah all the history of Israel, all that was vital in its priestly, prophetical and kingly institutions, was to culminate and to come to a focus, in order that from this new center salvation should be universally extended. In this historical sense Christ is the subject of Old Testament revelation.

All that pertains to the history of Israel as a divinely ordered factor in the salvation of the world, scripture including the divinely given Law and promises, has been deposited in the Old Testament Scriptures. They are more than a historical monument of the revelation of God in the old time. They are themselves a revelation of God for all time. In the New Testament they are recognized by Christ and the apostles as a divine means of grace for the guidance and instruction of the people of redemption.

CHAPTER VI
THE PERSON OF CHRIST
THE RESTORATION OF MAN TO COMMUNION WITH GOD REALIZED IN THE PERSON AND WORK OF CHRIST

THE NECESSITY OF A DIVINE HUMAN REDEEMER

When the communion of man with God was broken by sin, the realization of the divine purpose of redemption required a Mediator to bring God and man into union again. As sin was the cause of the alienation, the restoration of communion required a reconciliation by the removal of sin. The Mediator, who effected this reconciliation, had to represent in Himself both the human and the divine side.

The existence of sin made redemption necessary. The gracious will of God determined that the redemption should be effected by a reconciliation through a divine human Mediator. It is enough for us to know from the Scriptures that this is God's will. But it is satisfactory to our minds to see in some measure the reason for this form of God's purpose. Generally the necessity of a divine human Redeemer is explained from the atoning death of Christ. Redemption is viewed as a reconciliation of God's justice with His mercy, the former of which demanded the punishment of the sinner while the latter sought his pardon, and so God caused His Son to become man and to bear his punishment, in order that He could in mercy pardon without violating His justice. The essential truth of this conception, namely, that God's holiness forbids Him to compromise with sin even in exercising mercy, must be maintained. But it would be a mistake to

conceive of a tension between the righteousness and mercy
of God, as if they tended in opposite directions, and as if
God had to be reconciled with Himself. The righteousness of
God as well as His mercy demands the removal of sin; for the
existence of sin is as abhorrent to the righteousness of God
as the misery of the sinner is to His mercy. Another line of
thought proceeds from the incarnation as the union of the
divine with the human, and follows the conception that such
a union was necessary for the renewal of mankind in the
likeness of God. In the Mediator a new development of the
human race has its beginning, a development that runs
counter to the development in sin. Such a new development
could be brought about only by One who by the forgiveness
of sins could remove the burden of existing sin, and by new
impulses to holiness could inspire the love of righteousness.
No man could do this, least of all a sinful man. The Mediator
must be God, for He alone can give efficacy to the necessary
reconciliation, namely, bring pardon for sin and power for
righteousness; and He must be man, because a reconciliation
in which man does not participate has no validity for him.

Would God have become incarnate if man had not
sinned? In all periods of the history of the Church some
minds have answered this question in the affirmative. Back of
this question lies another, on the answer to which its decision
depends. Is the incarnation based upon metaphysical or
ethical necessity? Support for the metaphysical necessity of
the incarnation has been sought in those passages of the
Scriptures which assign to Christ a cosmic position, as in
Ephesians and Colossians; and also in the passages which
represent Christ as the second Adam. But inference from
such texts that the development of the world and of man
requires the incarnate presence of the Son of God is purely

speculative. It can have no weight against the concurrent teaching of the Bible that the only grounds for the incarnation are ethical. In the Scriptures the incarnation is predicated upon the existence of sin in the world. The whole revelation of God in Christ is declared to be for redemption, salvation and reconciliation. Cf. Mt 20:28: Jn 3:16, 12:47; 2 Co 5:19; 1 Tim 1:15. According to this plain and explicit teaching of Scripture sane theology has from ancient times rejected the useless speculation of an incarnation apart from sin.

CHRIST TRUE GOD AND TRUE MAN.

The Mediator required by the divine purpose of redemption appeared in the person of Jesus Christ, who though truly man was at the same time truly God.

The reality of the humanity and of the divinity known from the Bible of Jesus Christ can only be established by what the Scriptures say of Him. It is not possible to infer conclusively from the historical effects of Christianity or from the spirit of Christ in the world what kind of a person He was. We must go to the record contained in the Bible to see Jesus Christ as He is. Learning to know Him there, we can see Him reflected in historical effects.

The names by which the Redeemer is called in the Bible are significant, although no conclusive argument can be drawn from them alone. His personal name, Jesus, signifies Savior. Either a human or a divine being may be so designated. Christ, equivalent to the Old Testament Messiah, signifies the Anointed. It implies at least the possession of divine powers, especially as the name is applied to the

Redeemer fraught with Old Testament prophetic meanings. Son of Man is the designation by which Jesus generally spoke of Himself. Doubtless this is a Messianic name, based on Dan 7:13. If the name was originally Messianic, its signification in the New Testament is filled with a fuller content than is given in the Old Testament ideas. It was the mission of Jesus which really showed what the Son of Man is. As the name is realized in Jesus, it expresses universal relations to mankind. The designation must not, however, be diluted to the pale, abstract conception of the ideal man. It indicates perfect and universal humanity in Jesus with the implication that He was more than man. For it is used of Him not only in His humiliation, but also in His transcendent glory. Son of God refers to the divine origin of the Redeemer. This name has already been discussed under the head of the Trinity. Here let it be added that, although the designation comes over as a Messianic name from the Old Testament, as in Ps 2:7; 2 Sam 7:14, in the New Testament it becomes charged with a deeper meaning. It expresses perfection of sonship in relation to God. It describes Him who did not become, but was the Son of God. It is a designation of essential being, and not merely of office. Lord is applied to Christ in the apostolic writings in the same sense in which Jehovah is called Lord. It is a divine name.

These names indicate both true humanity and true divinity in the Redeemer. What they indicate is fully revealed in the portrait of Christ drawn in the Gospels. There is indeed a difference of coloring between the synoptists and St. John, the former giving more prominence to the human side of the life of Christ, the latter bringing out more conspicuously the divine features. But the human is not wanting in St. John nor the divine in the synoptists. The two

pictures are different but not discordant. It is not necessary
here to go far into the details of the evangelical picture of the
divine human person of Christ. The reality of His divinity has
already been discussed under the head of the Trinity, and the
principal proofs of it from the Gospels have there been
presented. The reality of the humanity is accentuated in many
details. Jesus passed through the ordinary stages of human
growth from birth to manhood, Lu 2 :40, 52 ; was subject to
the relations of human life, Lu 2:51; 8:3; had human needs, Jn
4:7;19:28; Mt 8:24; experienced human emotions, joy, Lu
10:21; love, Mk 10:21; Jn 11:5; compassion, Mt 9 :36 ; sorrow,
Mt 26 :38 ; Lu 19 :41 ; Jn 11:35; 12:27; 13:21; anger, Mk 3:5;
engaged in prayer, Mt 11:25; Mk 1:35; Jn 17:1.

The picture of Christ in the Gospels in His perfect
humanity and true divinity, the human traits so undisguisedly
portrayed while the whole man is transfigured with divine
glory, is corroborated by all the personal touches scattered
through the epistles and other apostolic utterances. The
divine elements have been sufficiently indicated in connection
with the Trinity. The human features are brought out in the
many references to His death and crucifixion; in the
designation of Him as man, Act 17:31 ; Ro 5:15 ; 1 Tim 2:5;
in the declaration of His birth, Ro 1:3; Gal 4:4; in His having
a body of flesh, Col 1:22; 1 P 3:18; 1 Jn 4:2; His sharing in
flesh and blood; Heb 2:14; His being in the likeness of sinful
flesh, Ro 8:3; His existing in weakness, 2 Co 13:4; His praying
and weeping, Heb 5:7; and in recognizing men as His
brethren, Heb 2:11.

Jesus was in every sense a true man, an individual
member of the human race, living at a definite time and in a
particular country, nationally a Jew. Still He was unique
among men. Two things especially distinguish Him from all

other men, and these two things are closely connected: His birth and His sinlessness. Though born like other men of a woman, a daughter of Israel of the line of David, the human origin of Jesus was due to a miraculous operation of the Holy Spirit, Mt 1:18sq.; Lu 1:26sq. The Son of Man was not the son of a man. By His miraculous birth Christ escaped the taint of sinfulness hereditary in the human race. The sinlessness of Christ is proved by the purity of His life. His challenge to be convicted of sin in Jn 8:46 is representative of His claim of freedom from sin and of His always doing the Father's will, Jn 4:34. He never prayed for forgiveness, although He urgently taught all others to do so. His sinlessness is implied in the entire unique relation of intimacy with the Father, in which He lived. In the apostolic writings He is always described as the One who delivers others from sin, the One therefore who has no sin, as is sometimes expressly declared of Him, 2 Co 5:21; Heb 4:15; 1 Pet 2:22.

The religious significance of the reality and completeness of the humanity of Christ lies in this, that in the reconciliation which He effected our humanity is represented, that mankind in Him is in perfect union with God, that in Him the human race has a new and perfect Head and is destined to become through Him a new creation.

The Church has in all ages jealously defended both the real humanity and true divinity of Christ. We have spoken of the divinity in another connection, so that we need only refer to His humanity here. Even before the close of the apostolic age the reality of Christ's humanity was denied by Gnostic teachers of docetism (the doctrine that Christ had only the appearance of humanity), who were vigorously opposed by St. John in his epistles and by subsequent early Christian writers. The completeness of the humanity of Christ was impugned by the Arians and by the talented anti-Arian, Apollinaris, who on both sides conceived of Christ as an incomplete man, inasmuch as the pre-existent Logos took the place of the higher rational faculty in Him. This error was strenuously opposed by orthodox theologians and various councils in the fourth and fifth centuries, notably the Council of Constantinople in 381. Since then the reality and completeness of the humanity of Christ have been fixed in the doctrine of the Church.

A subtle question affecting the conception of the complete humanity of Christ requires a few remarks here. Was Christ a human person? Or was His humanity impersonal? Traditional scholastic theology from the days of John of Damascus in the eighth century has decided in favor of the latter alternative. In order to exclude the idea that the incarnate Christ was a double person the Damascene invented the term "*enhypostasia*" and explained that the Son of God with His eternal personality assumed a human nature without "*hypostasis*" (personality), although possessed of consciousness and will. The "*hypostasis*" of the Son of God became that of the human nature also. This construction was fully adopted by the Lutheran theologians of the seventeenth century, who accordingly taught the "*anhypostasia*" of the human nature of Christ. To us the conception appears scholastic and artificial. But in weighing it the underlying intention to maintain the unity of the person of Christ must be fully appreciated. It is also necessary to remember that the scholastic term, *hypostasis* or subsistence, is not the precise equivalent of what we now call personality. To our minds personality is an integral element in the idea of a man. And Jesus was a man. John Gerhard questioned whether it ought to be said that "the Son of God assumed a man," although he acknowledged that this form of speech was the regular usage of the Church Fathers and that it was followed by eminent Lutheran writers. He admitted it only in the sense that "the Son of God assumed humanity." Frank is undoubtedly correct when he says : "However correct the premises were on which the construction of '*anhypostasia*' was built, the fact was overlooked, which of all is the most certain, that the person of the Mediator in the days of His earthly walk presented Himself as a human person." Thomasius says: "The picture of the Redeemer, as it lies before us in the Gospels, is the picture of a truly human personality, a truly human life, human in the fullest and finest sense of the word." No theological construction should twist so obvious a fact.

CHRIST ONE PERSON.

The Redeemer is true God and true man, but not in the parallel existence of a double person. He is one person, a person who is not simply divine nor simply human, but divine human. Hence He is correctly called the God-man.

When we speak of a person, we have in mind a being with a self-consciousness in which all the acts and experiences of a life are unified and by which the identity of the life is maintained. If there is anything fixed in the faith of the Christian and of the Church, it is the conviction that we have truly one Savior, not a double Redeemer existing in two distinct spheres of life and consciousness. But the knowledge of this truth has not its ultimate source in the experience of the Christian or the consciousness of the Church, but in the historical revelation of Christ recorded in the Scriptures. In the New Testament we can trace three concurrent lines of evidence for the personal unity of Christ: first, the unity of the life of Christ; secondly, the unity of consciousness manifest in all utterances of Christ about Himself; thirdly, the unity of personality ascribed to Him by all the writers of the New Testament.

The unity of the life of Jesus Christ is obvious to every reader of the Gospels. The marked difference in presentation between the synoptists and St. John does not destroy the natural impression of this unity. In none of the Gospel accounts, nor in the total view given by all taken together, does the life of Christ fall apart into divisions, one human, the other divine. It is often said with reference to some circumstance or act, that Jesus did this as man or this as God. But the Gospels do not say so. The manifestations of life are not apportioned to different sides of being in this way. It is one life. The unity of this life points back to a unity of personality, in whom the divine and human are indissolubly blended.

It is only a different aspect of the same essential fact that appears in the unity of consciousness in all Christ says of Himself. When reading His words, we never have the impression that now God is speaking apart from the man in Him, now the man alone. Even when His statements combine things most widely separated in human conception, the earthly and the heavenly, the present and the preexistent, they are the outflow of a single consciousness, which holds these most diverse things within itself. This is especially striking when He speaks from His position upon earth and in earthly relations and declares what pertains to His preexistence or to His unique relation to the Father. Nowhere is there a suggestion of a double consciousness or of a transition from one mode of personal life to another. It is always the same personal identity, the same Ego. As instances, we may refer to the way He thanks the Father for the knowledge granted to His disciples and immediately passes over to His own unique knowledge of the Father, Mt 11:25-27; to His claim to be the bread from heaven and to have power to ascend to heaven, Jn 6:33, 51, 62; or to His claim of unity with the Father, Jn 10:30 ; 14:10.

Observing the manner in which the writers of the New Testament refer to Christ, it must be borne in mind that for them He was the divine Lord, who nevertheless lived in an earthly life. But they always conceived of Him as one person. Whether His preexistence or His divine glory, or whether His earthly life and events in it are referred to, it is always the same personal subject who is spoken of. Occasionally this unity of personality is expressly asserted, 1 Co 8:6; 1 Tim 2:5.

In accordance with the Scripture representation of the person of Christ the Church has expressed its faith for all ages in the Nicene Creed: "I believe in one Lord Jesus Christ."

But how can one person be at the same time true God and true man? This is the great Christological problem with which theology has wrestled during the entire history of the Christian Church. At this point a reminder of the difference between the Christian faith and a theological construction of a doctrine is timely. The faith of the Church rests upon the teaching of the Word of God, and not upon the possibility of a logical and systematic arrangement and explanation of the revealed facts. It is proper and useful for theology to endeavor to give systematic expression in terms of human knowledge to the verities embraced in the faith of the Church. But if it does not succeed in its endeavor, nevertheless the faith stands upon the foundation of revealed truth. Theology has its problems, although the faith which it seeks to explain is not problematic. Among the problems which theology has never yet adequately explained, the person of Christ furnishes one of the greatest.

THE PERSONAL UNION.

God and man are so united in Christ as to form one person. This is called the personal union. The mode of this union is generally and correctly described as an assuming of humanity by the preexistent Son of God in such form that no mixture of the divine and human natures occurred and that neither the divine nor the human nature has undergone any essential change. On the other hand, there is so complete a reciprocal interpenetration of the human and divine, that neither acts or exists apart from the other.

It is customary to speak of the two sides of the person of Christ as the two natures. The word nature is here used in the sense of the "essence of any particular being or class of beings, that which makes it what it is." In thinking of the union of the divine and human in Christ it is important to guard against the misconceptions which arise from analogies of the union, mechanical or chemical, of physical substances. Every conception of the union of two substances to form a third substance must be rigidly excluded. Another caution necessary for the student is that we must not think of the two natures as two complete materials or two finished things, which are brought into a unity of being. The Son of God is indeed complete in His being from eternity, but He is not a material. He is life, personal being. The human nature came into being in the incarnation. It is also personal life, developed, perfected and glorified in the personal union with the divine, not a material.

In attempting to form some conception of the personal union of the divine and human in Christ, we must be deeply sensible that we are trying to reduce to forms of thought that which necessarily in large measure transcends all human thought. The fact is a fact of revelation, which remains true when all theories to explain it remain inadequate.

The Bible declares the fact of the incarnation. In the Gospels it presents the personal life of the incarnate One in its operation, and in the epistles in its effects. But we must not expect to find a theoretical explanation of the mystery of the personal union of God and man in Christ. The narratives of the birth of Christ in St. Matthew and St. Luke confine themselves to an account of the miraculousness of that birth. The nearest approach to a theoretical statement is found in Jn 1:14: "The Word became flesh and dwelt among us." But in reality it is a declaration of the fact of the incarnation, and not of its inner secret. The word "became" is a general indefinite term, and the word "dwelt," "tabernacled" expresses the manifestation of the divine life in Christ, not the mode of its union with His humanity. The same is true of 1 Tim 3 :16 and Gal 4 :4. The declaration in 1 Jn 4 :2, "Jesus Christ is come in the flesh," emphasizes the reality of the human being of Christ in the incarnation. The passage Phil 2:7 is supposed by many to refer to the act of the incarnation, and an elaborate theory of the incarnation, the Kenotic theory, is built chiefly upon the word "emptied himself," but we believe with incorrect exegesis. The apostle is not speaking of the act of the incarnation, but of the modality of the life of the incarnate One upon earth in lowliness, sorrow and pain, just as in Ro 8:3 he declares that "God sent His Son in the likeness of sinful flesh." The likeness of the flesh of sin means human being as conditioned by sin, subject to the evils and sorrows consequent upon sin, hence also including death. So we find Christ described in Heb 2:14 as a partaker of humanity, "flesh and blood," and so also of death. The mystery of the incarnation is presented in living reality in the New Testament. The explanation of that mystery must be arrived at by inference from the facts exhibited in the dual life, divine and human, in Christ, which is yet not a double life, but a unified personal life.

To express the idea of the incarnation it has been customary since the early centuries of the Church to speak of it as an assumption of the human nature by the divine. The word "assumed" is a suitable word, and has scriptural analogues, as in Heb 2:16: "He taketh hold of the seed of Abraham." It is well adapted to bring out the truth that in the incarnation the initiative was on the part of the eternal Son of God, personally existing. The incarnation was nothing like a man growing up into godlikeness. The word "assumed" is in important respects a suitable word for the incarnation, yet it is inadequate. One may assume a dress, an office, a form of life, which may be dropped again. Here we have personal and enduring union. The conception of assumption, applied to the personal union in Christ, still leaves room for dualistic ideas. Indeed it suggests the conception of a lower human life and a higher divine life hovering over it with its penetrating influences. To overcome this dualism in the conception of the personal union and to lay hold of the idea of a unified person, it is necessary to define the idea of assumption further so as to remove every element of mere besideness of the divine and human natures and of separation between them. In homely phrase it may be said, they are all in each other. The acts of Christ cannot be referred separately to the human and divine natures. All, however human the manifestation of the action or however divine it may appear, all is personal and theanthropic. Behind this interpenetration in action lies the interpenetration in existence. The divine and the human natures exist in unity in Christ. They do not merely coincide in a limited circle, outside of which the person has life that is only human, and again in boundless sweep life that is only divine. Incidentally let it be remarked that the characteristic feature of Luther's christology is his insistence upon the perfect unity of the life of Christ. In this lies his advance upon earlier christology. He sang: "He whom the world could not in wrap yonder lies in Mary's lap; He is become an infant small, who by His might upholdeth all."

But this intimate personal union is not transformation of one nature into the other nor absorption of one by the other. The Son of God was not turned into a man nor the man Jesus into a god. The essence and attributes of both divinity and humanity are preserved. Of course there is no analogy in the world for such a unique personal union. But something like what the German poet dreamed is here fact and reality: "Two souls and one thought, two hearts and one beat."

In endeavoring to visualize mentally the person in the perfect union of His two natures it is best to begin with the unity of His consciousness, manifest in His self-revelation. Nowhere in the Scriptures is there an indication that Christ made a personal differentiation between the human and divine in Himself, as He differentiates between Himself and the Father, with whom He nevertheless claimed to be one. There is no evidence of a break or transition in His consciousness at the incarnation. It is the same "I" unincarnate and incarnate. The eternal Son of God has not undergone a change by which He ceased to be in any respect what He was. The incarnation was indeed a change in the modality of His being, but it produced no alteration in His divine existence either as to His essence or attributes. The modern theory of Kenosis, of which we shall speak later, does introduce an alteration in the divine attributes in the incarnation, but that theory must be rejected. The unity of consciousness in Christ shows that the consciousness of the Son of God has taken up into unity with itself the consciousness of a man, so that now there is one divine-human consciousness, and that forever. We remember here that Jesus was never a man outside of the personal union with God, that His personal human life was formed and perfected in the personal life of the preexistent Son of God. From the incarnation the center of the personal life was a point of coincidence of true divine and true human life.

One of the chief difficulties in Christology is to conceive of Christ in such a way as not to give the human life of Him an appearance of unreality. But a divine human consciousness does not contradict the most human experience of Jesus. The human features in Him are manifestations of an infinite divine fullness of life. Christ on earth did not give forth infinite displays of power, knowledge and majesty. Even His miracles were exhibitions of supernatural power in finite form, not exhibitions of omnipotence. His life on earth stood in real correlation with the finite forces of the world. But behind the finite about Him, or rather pervading it, was the infinite. The human was rooted and grounded in the divine. Jesus always acted with the consciousness of an infinite reserve power, which is especially evident in His marvelous self-restraint. He exerted at every moment so much knowledge and power of life as the moment demanded. He was truly a child, truly a man in humility and glory, and yet He always was the Son of God.

But was there not in Christ a double consciousness, one human and the other divine, in perfect accord perhaps, the human always subordinated to the divine, yet two centers of personality? The formula of the Council of Constantinople of 680 suggests such an idea, although it asserts one person and one subsistence. The formula declares:

> "We declare that in Him are two natural wills and two natural operations. And these two natural wills are not contrary the one to the other, but His human will follows and that not as resisting or reluctant, but rather as subject to His divine and omnipotent will."

This statement leaves some things in the personal union unexplained. It does not carry us back to the center of unified consciousness of Christ. But closely examined, it does not assert two centers of personality in Christ (that would have been declared Nestorian heresy by that Council) but the coincidence of the human will with the divine. The coincidence of the human consciousness with the divine is not a double consciousness, but a unified consciousness. It is one selfhood. The consciousness of Christ was one, but the mental states of Christ were not always one and the same. Jesus slept and then His mind was not wide awake. So we need not be surprised that He professed ignorance in regard to a fact, Mk 13:32. But when it was necessary to know, Jesus always knew without being informed by man; for in His personality were infinite depths.

Therefore we fully recognize a true human development in Christ, but always in the unity of a theanthropic consciousness. In infancy the thoughts were those of a babe, in youth the thoughts of a youth, in manhood the thoughts of a man, and in glory after the resurrection the thoughts of the Son of man in glory. The circle of thinking, willing and acting widens with the growth of Christ from the manger to the throne at the right hand of God; but in all stages the human thoughts rest upon the infinite bosom of the eternal thoughts of the Son of God and vibrate in unison with them.

COMMUNION OF THE TWO NATURES.

The personal union of the divine and human natures in Christ includes a relation of communion between the two natures. The divine nature completely dwells in the human nature and permeates it so that both are brought into the unity of personal life, and neither exists apart from the other. The Son of God in the entirety of His divine essence has become incarnate.

The union of God and man in one person could not be without a conjunction of the two natures which constitute the unity. But to define the character of this conjunction has ever been a problem. These limits are set by the very nature of the person of Christ: the conjunction must be such that the personal life does not fall asunder into a double life; and it must be such that one nature shall not be absorbed by the other. The ancient Church in its wrestlings with the problem arrived at a fixation of these limits in the rule of the council of Chalcedon in 451. That rule is: "One person of the Lord in two natures, unconfused, unchanged, unseparated, undivided." The unity of the person was affirmed in opposition to Nestorianism, which conceived of the two natures as existing separately without real conjunction, each concurring according to its powers in the acts of the person, so disrupting the unity of the person. The integrity of the two natures was affirmed in opposition to the Eutychian or monophysite error, which conceived the human nature as transformed into a deified nature, so that Christ's humanity was unlike our humanity. A sound christology will always abide within the limits of the Chalcedon rule. But theology cannot stop there. Lutheran theology has made an advance beyond the theological inheritance of the ancient Church in the direction of affirming a more vital conjunction, a more perfect interpenetration of the two natures.

That in the personal union in Christ there is a conjunction of the natures is evident. But what kind of a conjunction is it? First of all it is not a conjunction of things equal. The divine nature is the giving nature; the human nature is the receiving nature. But the human nature is not merely passive like an inanimate object. The human nature is a man with life. Therefore the conjunction is not physical, but vital. One person means a common life of the two natures. In this vital union each nature is modified and determined by the other, not in its essence or attributes, but its relations. The Son of God now lives only as the incarnate One. The man Jesus lives only as the God-man. Hence the proposition must be laid down, that neither nature exists apart from the other.

This proposition Lutheran theology has labored to uphold. In doing so it has encountered the opposition of Reformed theology, which is unwilling to carry the conjunction of the two natures to the extent which Lutheran theology defends. "Neither the Logos outside of the flesh, nor the flesh outside of the Logos." This rule of the old Lutheran theologians was opposed to what they called the "Calvinistic extra"(*extra Calvinisticum*). For Reformed theology affirmed a total indwelling of the Logos in the human nature, but held also that the Logos is also entirely without (*extra*) the human nature. The basis of its doctrine is the absolute difference between the essence of God and that of man. It is absolutely governed by the principle, *finitum non est capax infiniti*, the finite cannot take up the infinite. Lutheran theology on the other hand discovers the very mystery of the incarnation in the principle, *humana natura in Christa capax est divinae*, the human nature can take up the divine nature. It maintains a real communion of the two natures, and not a mere fellowship between them as Reformed theology tends to affirm.

From the beginning there has always been a difference among Lutheran theologians in regard to the application of the principle of the communion of natures. A more recent development is the Kenotic theory, which teaches that in the incarnation the Son of God adjusted Himself to the limits of a truly human life by a self-limitation, a Kenosis of the divine nature, according to which it retained its essence, but reduced its operative attributes to a condition of potency. Such a limitation of divine attributes is scarcely conceivable, and if it were, it would imply a change that would infringe upon the immutability of God and seriously interfere with the trinitarian relations in the Godhead. Nor is such an idea necessary to safeguard the true humanity of Christ. Why cannot the divine life of the Son of God continue as it is while it exhibits itself in the form of human life? Kenoticism objects that then the personal life of Christ exists in a double mode of being. But that is not a double life, but two sides of the same personal life.

To give expression to the reality of the communion of the two natures older theology noted what they called the "personal propositions." They affirmed that such propositions as, "God is man," "Jesus is God," are literally true in the person of Christ. But what is true in this one concrete instance is not true of the two natures in the abstract. It cannot be said that humanity is divinity in Christ.

THE COMMUNICATION OF PROPERTIES.

The personal union in Christ is more accurately defined by the doctrine of the communication of properties. The properties and works of Christ, whether per se human or divine, are not to be limited to each nature respectively, but are the properties and works of the person. Moreover, as the natures are in communion, the human nature shares in the properties of the divine.

This doctrine, technically called *communicatio idiomatum*, was derived from ancient theology, but received a new and peculiar development in the Lutheran Church.

The specifications of the reciprocal relations of the two natures under it are only nearer definitions of the unity of the divine human person of Christ. It is usual to distinguish three kinds, which will be briefly described with examples from the New Testament.

In the first place, human properties are ascribed to Christ designated by divine names. "Killed the Prince of life," Act 3:15. "Crucified the Lord of Glory," 1 Co 2:8. "The Son of God gave Himself up for me," Gal 2:20. Conversely, divine properties are ascribed to Christ designated by human names. "The Son of man ascending where He was before," Jn 6:62. "The second man is of heaven," 1 Co 15:47. Sometimes both human and divine properties are ascribed to Christ designated by a name both human and divine. "Of whom is Christ as concerning the flesh, who is over all, God blessed forever," Ro 9:5. "He was crucified through weakness, yet He liveth through the power of God," 2 Co 13:4. Now in all such instances the Scriptures do not admit of sundering of the person by making what is human applicable only to the human nature, and what is divine applicable only to the divine nature. The properties of either nature are the properties of the person. This is the first kind of communication of properties, technically called the *Idiomatic Genus*.

In the second place, the works of redemption are referred to the person, designated by either human or divine names, and not to the natures separately. "The church of the Lord which He purchased with His own blood," Act 20:28. "Christ died for our sins," 1 Co 15:3. "One mediator between God and man, Himself man, Christ Jesus, who gave Himself a ransom for all," 1 Tim 2:5. In such statements it is an abuse of abstraction to refer what is human only to the human nature and what is divine only to the divine nature. The redemptive operations must be ascribed to the person, and not exclusively to one or the other nature, as for example, death to the human nature only. This also is a kind of communication of properties. The Greek word "*apotelesmata*" was formerly used to designate the redemptive operations of Christ. Hence this kind of communication, by which the redemptive works are ascribed to the person, is called the *Apotelesmatic Genus*.

In the third place, divine attributes are predicated of Christ in such a way that it follows that as man He shares in divine prerogatives. "The Son of man hath authority on earth to forgive sins," Mt 9:6. "All things have been delivered unto me of my Father, ' Mt 11 :27. "All authority hath been given unto me in heaven and on earth," Mt 28:18. "He gave Him authority to execute judgment," Jn 5:27. "He is able to subject all things unto Himself," Phil 3:21. "Ascended far above all the heavens, that He might fill all things," Eph 4:10. Christ is declared to be at the right hand of God, which implies omnipresence. Full justice is not done to such declarations by attributing to the human nature of Christ only extraordinary, but limited powers, while the divine properties are exclusively restricted to the divine nature, as Reformed theology demands. Such utterances show that the human nature participates in the glories of the divine, that is, the attributes of the divine nature are in their operation shared in by the human nature. This also is communication of properties, and as the word majesty embraces the divine glories and properties, this form is called the *Majestatic Genus*.

This doctrine of the communication of properties was the subject of bitter controversy between the Lutheran and Reformed theologians of the sixteenth century, especially the *Majestatic Genus*, which the Reformed vehemently antagonized. What lent practical interest to the dispute was its connection with the question of the presence of the Lord's body in the Holy Supper. The doctrine in its Lutheran form originated with Luther. It was not developed on the same lines in subsequent Lutheran theology. John Brenz became the father of a thoroughgoing doctrine of the divine exaltation of the humanity of Christ, Martin Chemnitz of a modified doctrine of its exaltation. For example, Brenz taught the actual omnipresence of Christ's body in a supernatural way; Chemnitz taught a multivolipresence, a presence of Christ's body where He willed it to be.

A few special remarks may prevent misunderstandings in regard to the *Majestatic Genus*. It is a communication from nature to nature. The *Idiomatic* and the *Apotelesmatic genera* are communication from the natures to the person. Here the attributes of the divine nature are communicated to the human nature. It is not a transfusion, by which the divine essence parts with something in it, or the essence of the humanity is changed. The humanity always remains in itself finite. The communication of the divine attributes is not such as to produce an infinite expansion of the human nature. It only imparts to it the ability to concur and participate in the divine works of Christ. The attribute most under discussion, on account of the Lord's Supper, was omnipresence. But this omnipresence is illocal, beyond the limits and laws of space, as is the omnipresence of God. The communication of divine attributes to the human nature is not absolute. The divine attributes do not become the attributes of the human nature. This shares in them. The divine powers of the Son of God are operative through His humanity. The *Majestatic Genus* underlies the divine human mediatorial work of Christ. It is grounded in the personal union. It begins with the beginning of the incarnation, not with the resurrection. It is the expression of the truth of the union of man with God, of the fact that the life of man has been lifted up into the life of God.

The modern Kenotic theory requires that there shall be a fourth kind of communication of *Idiomata*, a *genus* of humiliation, according to which the human attributes are communicated to the divine nature during the Lord's earthly life. Older Lutheran theology, in fact the Formula of

Concord, expressly rejected such a communication as in conflict with the immutability of the divine nature. On this ground and on other grounds we think the Kenotic theory is a mistaken effort to explain the mystery of Christ's person.

THE STATES OF CHRIST.

By the act of incarnation Christ became all that He was, the God-man. The changes of condition in His subsequent life neither subtracted from nor added to His being. His life as the incarnate One was for a time historical; it then became supramundane, but has continued operative in this world, although He is unseen. To indicate this difference in the condition of Christ on earth and above the world, a distinction is made between the two states of humiliation and exaltation. Both of these states are predicated of the incarnate Christ. The incarnation itself was not the humiliation. The state of humiliation embraces all those experiences of abasement and suffering in the earthly life of Christ that stood in contrast with the divine glory of His person. The state of exaltation embraces those experiences in which His glory is manifested in power and majesty on earth and in heaven.

The distinction of two states of Christ is based upon what St. Paul says in Phil 2:5-11. Here the apostle distinguishes the condition in which Christ "emptied Himself," from the succeeding condition in which God "highly exalted Him." It is important to note that when he says, "He emptied Himself," the apostle is speaking of the incarnate Christ and not, as is so often supposed, of the act of the incarnation. He is presenting the humility of Christ as an example for imitation. For this the incarnation would not be suitable. But St. Paul refers to the well-known humble, self-denying life of Jesus on earth which terminated with the crucifixion. He says that Jesus, without grasping what did not belong to Him, could at any moment have lived in divine glory; but He voluntarily refrained from this and chose the vicissitudes of common human experience, nay more, the life of a bondservant and the criminal's death. This self-renunciation God honored and undid all the disgrace of the humiliation by placing Him where His inherent dignity, that excels all other dignities, must be universally acknowledged. So God highly exalted Him, not by making Him divine (He was that), but by bringing His glory and majesty into display and recognition, just as the apostle declares that God's Son, who was born of the seed of David humanly, was constituted the Son of God with power by the resurrection, Ro 1:4. The same idea is more briefly expressed by St. Paul, when, holding up Christ as an example of self-denial, he says: "Ye know the grace of our Lord Jesus Christ, that, though He was rich, yet for your sakes He became poor," 2 Co 8:9. Christ did not become poor by becoming incarnate, but being incarnate He chose the life of poverty, although He was rich. The same idea of humiliation followed by exaltation is found in Heb 12:2, where it is said that Jesus, for the joy that was set before Him, endured the cross, despising the shame, and sat down at the right hand of the throne of God.

The principal stages in the humiliation and exaltation of Christ are indicated in the Apostles' Creed. The humble birth, the self-denying life, the passion, the ignominious death and the burial, mark the humiliation. The descent into hell, the resurrection, the ascension and the seat at the right hand of God mark the exaltation.

No little difficulty is connected with the conception of these states of Christ. The problem is to maintain the reality of the human life of Jesus, both on earth and in His ascended state in heaven, together with the reality of His divine majesty. This problem leads right back into the depths of the question of the incarnation. What effect had the incarnation on the humanity of Christ? What effect on His divinity? The explanation, according to the best traditions of Lutheran theology, is that the divine nature, being immutable, is subject neither to humiliation nor exaltation. Therefore the effect of the incarnation upon the divine nature was simply to join the human nature to it. But by the communication of properties the human nature from the beginning of the incarnation shares in the majesty, in the attributes of the divine. The effect of the incarnation is to glorify the human nature. But, making a distinction between possession and use, it is claimed that Christ abstained from the exercise, according to His human nature, of the communicated divine attributes for a time, meanwhile exercising His attributes divinely only (this is the humiliation), and then brought them into full exercise also according to his human nature (this is the exaltation).

In the main this explanation is doubtless correct. But it is not altogether satisfying. It creates the impression that the humiliation and the exaltation are experiences of only the human nature and that Christ's life is not a unified life. Moreover, the human life of Christ appears like a mechanical process carried out with mutations as circumstances require. Besides this, there is difficulty in conceiving the reality of the possession of divine attributes that are unexercised; for instance, omniscience that does not know all is not omniscience.

The truth that the states of Christ are not only states of the human nature, but of the entire person, must be earnestly carried through. These states affect the divine nature also. In Christ God suffered and rejoiced in His glory. This does not destroy the immutability of God. As we see it, it is necessary to break through the idea of the absolute difference between the essence of God and of man. As living personalities God and man are akin. Man is capable of receiving divine life. God is capable of entering into human life. The finite and the infinite are not mutually exclusive. God's whole relation to a finite created world shows that this is not the case. In Christ the divine and the human are vitally united, that is, they have one personal life, at once divine and human. This one personal life manifests itself in operations divine and in operations human, and both kinds of operation now in humiliation and now in glory. By the personal union the human nature always participates in the divine life of majesty, not in infinite operations of its own, of which it is incapable, but in such a way that its finite operations are indissolubly connected with the divine operations in the universe, are, so to speak, of a piece with them, and in such a way that they are capable of an unlimited intensity of power and effect. Back of every finite act of Jesus is the plenitude of divine power and majesty, and this is put into exercise through His humanity as Christ wills. What Luther said with reference to the death of Christ applies to His every state, whether of abasement or of glory : "What is said of Him as man, that must be said also of God, namely, Christ died and Christ is God, therefore God died."

The change from a state of humiliation to a state exaltation added nothing to Christ. It did not make Him greater. It only manifested His great ness more completely. The idea of a gradual incarnation, worked out with such depth of learning and speculation by Dorner, cannot be accepted. It was the constitution of Christ's person in the act of incarnation which made His greatness. But the manifestation of His glory was gradual, as in His life there was real development. The Risen One was not greater than the babe in Bethlehem, but what He was was made manifest by the resurrection and by every step in His exaltation from the time when St. John first beheld His glory, the glory of the only begotten of the Father, and before.

The Kenotic theory has already been referred to. Its special design was to explain the states of Christ, more particularly the truly human development of His earthly life. The aim is commendable, but the line of thinking, notwithstanding its wide popularity, is unsound. To reduce the divine nature by self -limitation to the dimensions of a human life is to make Christ's divinity for the time being merely potential. A human Christ with mere potential divinity in his soul is not the God-man in whom all the fullness of the Godhead dwells bodily, even if the potential divinity afterwards burst out into actuality carrying the humanity with it into its divine glories.

Out of the Christology of Luther divergent tendencies arose, which developed sharp contrasts in the sixteenth century and open controversy in the seventeenth century. The Christology of Luther affirmed the truest humanity and the fullest divinity of Christ in complete union and communion. In this most intimate union of the divine and human natures Luther conceived the human nature as existing in a double mode of being, a natural and a supernatural. The humanity lived in the limitations of time and earthly relations, and at the same time participated in a heavenly way in the omnipotence, omnipresence and all the attributes of God. It had at once a local mode of existence, like any man, and an illocal mode of existence like God.

Christ, according to His humanity, was at once on earth and in heaven. In this realistic Christology Luther did not reflect much upon the difference of the states of Christ. As soon as this difference became the subject of theological discussion, a divergence among Lutheran theologians showed itself as to the extent to which Christ actually exercised His divine attributes, according to His human nature, during His humiliation. Pupils of John Brenz led the way in developing the view that from the incarnation Christ fully exercised all the communicated divine attributes, but in a hidden way. Martin Chemnitz developed the view that Christ divested the human nature of its communicated divine properties during His humiliation. The human nature retained the possession of them, but abstained from their use. This divergence does not appear in the Formula of Concord, although representatives of both views were engaged in its preparation. But early in the seventeenth century the two views clashed. The controversy between the theologians of Tubingen and of Giessen was arbitrated by the theologians of Saxony with the decision in favor of the view of Chemnitz. But it must be acknowledged that Chemnitz bent Luther's Christology towards the Calvinistic *extra carnem*, operations of the divine nature apart from the humanity of Christ.

CHAPTER VII
THE WORK OF CHRIST
THE RESTORATION OF MAN TO COMMUNION WITH GOD REALIZED IN THE PERSON AND WORK OF CHRIST

REDEMPTION

The work of Christ is the restoration of man to communion with God by a redemption from sin in all its aspects: its guilt, its power, and its penalty. The redemption of man consists primarily in the transferring of him from the state of alienation into a new relation of grace towards God through the mediation of Christ, in which new relation man is also spiritually transformed and glorified.

The word redemption is not always used in the same sense in theology or in the Scriptures. The general idea is that of deliverance. In the Old Testament it refers to deliverance from ills generally. In the New Testament its use is restricted to a religious sense, sometimes with special reference to the work of Christ by which forgiveness of sins is obtained, Ro 3:24 ; Eph 1:7; Col 1:14. Sometimes the word applies to the final deliverance from all the evils of this world, Ro 8:23; Eph 4:30. In theological usage there is a similar fluctuation in the narrower or wider application of the term. The word is here used in its comprehensive sense, as it is used in Luther's Catechism to describe the significance of the contents of the second article of the Apostles' Creed.

Biblical conceptions of redemption all presuppose some kind of a state of bondage, whether in bodily or moral ills. In the Old Testament the deliverance from physical evils bulks very largely, because physical evils, both individual and national, were viewed as evidences that the fellowship with

God was disturbed. The word redemption is generally applied to the people collectively, especially in relation to the surrounding hostile nations. In a signal way the deliverance from the bondage of Egypt was the redemption. Cf. Act 7:35. In prophecy the term especially refers to deliverance from the Babylonian exile, but the national deliverance is to be accompanied by a great, final, spiritual redemption. In the final redemption God Himself will come as the Redeemer, who not only sets His people free from the oppressions of the hostile nations, but also transforms them spiritually. The end is a state of perfection in which all evils shall have an end and all sins be overcome. This redemption is also to be effected by the promised Messiah. In the Old Testament Jehovah as redeemer and the Messiah as redeemer are not yet identified, although it is one work of redemption. This identification is made in the New Testament.

This promised redemption of Israel devout Jews were waiting for at the beginning of the New Testament, Luke 1:68; 2:38; 24:21. In the progress of the New Testament the conception of redemption which was brought over from the Old Testament, was advanced in three respects. First, the religious element, the relation to the remission of sins, was put in the foreground. Secondly, the physical redemption was made to recede to the last times, so becoming eschatological. Thirdly, the death of Christ, as the means of procuring redemption, was made the central and significant feature. All this will appear in the references which follow. Jesus revealed Himself as the Redeemer by His healing works of deliverance, which had more than a physical significance. Cf. Luke 4:16-21; Mt 11:4-6. He declared that He gave His life as a ransom for many, Mt 20:28, and that He laid it down for the sheep, Jn 10:15, not specifying sin, but implying it among the evils from which He brought deliverance. He also declared that the redemption would draw nigh when He returned, Lu 21:28. St. Paul points to the remission of sins as the very heart of redemption and connects it with the death of Christ. Cf. Eph 1:7; Col 1:14; Ro 3:24. He calls the death of Christ the ransom, 1 Tim 2:6, the means to redeem us from all iniquity, Tit 2:14. He sees in Christ's subjection to the law with its condemnation for sin the redemption of men from the curse of the law, Gal 3:13; 4:5. Those who believe in Christ are His possession, purchased with a price, 1 Co 6:20; 7:23. But, on the other hand, St. Paul looks for the final redemption from all evils of the sin-cursed world at the return of Christ, Ro 8:23; Eph 4:30. St. Peter speaks of Christ's disciples as bought by him, 2 Pet 2:1, and designates as the price of redemption His sacrificial blood, 1 Pet 1:18-19.

According to this biblical teaching redemption is deliverance from evil generally, but as all evil is related to sin as its source, redemption is liberation from sin in all its aspects, its guilt, its dominion and its penalty or consequent pains. So Luther describes the redemption of Christ in the Small Catechism: "Redeemed me from all sin, from death and the power of the devil, that I might be His own and live under Him in everlasting righteousness, innocence and blessedness." Redemption begins with the removal of guilt, the forgiveness of sins. Freedom from the dominion of sin follows, and finally redemption is completed in the termination of all evils.

In view of the tendency of the human mind to find the ground of redemption somehow in the conduct of man, it is important to observe that redemption is primarily a changed relation between God and man, which has been brought about by Christ and brought to man from God through Him. It is first of all remission of sins. It is not a change in the thoughts and affections of the human heart; it is not repentance and conversion. This change in the heart of man is the result of the redemption of Christ. Liberation from the guilt, dominion and penalty of sin is attended with an inner change in man, which begins with faith in Christ who has redeemed us, and which is inwardly effected by the Holy Spirit whom Christ gives to believers in Him. But this inner change is only the appropriation of the redemption of Christ, not the redemption itself nor its ground. The redemption of Christ has established a new relation between God and man, which expresses itself in the forgiveness of sins. "Where there is forgiveness of sins, there also are life and salvation." Because there is no condemnation to those who are in Christ Jesus, the dominion of sin and the consequences of sin, namely death and other punishments, are in principle broken and destroyed by the redemption of Christ, which has brought the remission of sins.

Redemption is a divine work of Christ effected from within the human race, in His own person as well as a work of love, but it is not a work of force. It is not performed by Christ standing over the world as an absolute Lord and working changes in it by His power. He has redeemed humanity from within the human race, in His own person bearing the sin of the world and realizing the relation of fellowship and union with God and drawing men into it. He is the second Adam, the redeemer who is God incarnate. He is the author of a new development of mankind. To use the terminology of Frank, the mankind of God is posited in the God-man; the mankind of God grows out of the God-man.

ATONEMENT

Christ redeemed the world by an atonement, that is, a work by which God and man, who were alienated by sin, were again brought into agreement. To make atonement Christ did that which was necessary to enable God without prejudice to His moral nature to forgive lost and condemned sinners their sins and to receive them again as His sons.

In this summary paragraph very general terms were designedly used, so as not to introduce a theory of the atonement before the facts on which the theory is to be based were brought out. There is so much that enters into the discussion of the atonement that the matter will be broken up into a number of short sections.

For the present the word atonement is used in its primary sense of bringing into agreement. Even the word reconciliation is for the present avoided, because varying conceptions are attached to this New Testament word. Much less has that ordinary meaning of atonement, namely, expiation, been introduced here, so as not to decide in advance that the atonement of Christ is a work of expiation. But while we have used the word atonement in as colorless a sense as was possible, it is not possible to discuss the subject without taking into consideration the cause of disagreement between God and man. That cause is man's sin. The atonement of Christ overcame the alienating effects of sin. This could not be without establishing a ground on which man might enjoy the forgiveness of sins. Now it is the opinion of many that man can enjoy this forgiveness as soon as he trusts God, who without further ado is able and ready to forgive sins at any time. The work of atonement then would be simply the making of the necessary impression upon men to lead them to believe God's forgiveness. But this opinion is based upon a misconception of the moral nature of God. If God's holiness means anything, it means that He reacts energetically against sin. Something must be done to satisfy the holy nature of God before He can accept sinners. From this premise the atonement of Christ, before it is an assurance to men that God will forgive them, must be the establishment of those conditions upon which God can in consistency with His moral nature exercise forgiveness. In Christ (we will not yet go into details as to His life or death), in Christ there is the ground not only for believing that God forgives, but of His forgiveness.

The doctrine of the atonement was never developed in the heat and logical determination of epochal controversies in the Church like the doctrine of the person of Christ. But the interest in the great Trinitarian and Christological controversies has always been at bottom to understand Christ as one who could make atonement. The doctrine of the atonement was gradually developed in the progress of theology. Although it is not incorrect to speak of an orthodox doctrine of atonement, the crystallization of certain fundamental ideas which have been woven into the doctrinal system of the largest part of Christendom, nevertheless there have been great variations of theological opinion in regard to the subject in all ages of the Church. Two fundamental types of conception run through the history of theology, and all theories of the atonement stand for the one or the other of these types or waver between them. These two types may be characterized as the subjective view of moral influence and the objective view of vicarious satisfaction. The fundamental question at issue is whether the work of Christ brought about any change of attitude in God in His relations to man, or whether a change is effected only in man's attitude towards God, no change in God being necessary.

Our study of the Bible has led us to decide in favor of the former alternative. The contrast of view here referred to came out clearly in two representatives of scholasticism in the Middle Ages. At the end of the eleventh century Anselm, in his famous book *Cur Deus Homo*, developed the theory that a vicarious legal satisfaction must be offered to God, whose Majesty has been injured by sin, before He can forgive sin. This satisfaction was rendered in the death of Christ. A generation later Abelard taught that the death of Christ is the revelation of God's infinite love, which revelation awakens in us love to God in return. The doctrine of Luther and of the Lutheran confessions is in the line of Anselm's teaching.

ATONEMENT IN THE OLD TESTAMENT

Under the old covenant atonement for sins was made by sacrifices and also by other means. These methods reveal that atonement proceeds from God, that it consists in an averting of the anger of God, and that in sacrificial atonement an innocent life goes for the guilty life. The biblical conception of the atonement of Christ cannot be determined by Old Testament ideas of atonement alone, for there are distinctive developments in the New Testament. But the New Testament doctrine of atonement grows out of the Old Testament conceptions. In order to understand how the idea of atonement was realized by Christ, it is necessary to note the lines of thought that run through the preparatory revelation contained in the Old Testament.

It should be noted carefully at the outset that the Old Testament conceptions of atonement are not all to be derived from the sacrificial institutions of the old covenant.

Important truths are found outside of the application of these sacrificial institutions. There is an extra-ritual atonement in the Old Testament. And it becomes especially important when it is remembered that the ritual atonement applies only to those who are already in God's covenant. It was atonement for inadvertent offences. Sins with a high hand, willful, defiant transgressions put the offender out of the covenant, outside of the sphere of God's grace, unless God granted a special atonement to restore him. Now when we come to the atonement of Christ, we must remember that those who receive its benefits are not persons that are already in the covenant of grace, but such as are brought into it by that very atonement. Therefore we will find that not only the Levitical sacrifices, but also the sacrifice by which the old covenant was instituted, Ex 24:5, and the extraordinary atonements in the Old Testament influenced New Testament conceptions.

The fundamental fact that the ritual sacrifices of the old covenant were for those already in the covenant and communion of God, throws some light upon the significance of these rites, about which there has been much diversity of view. Those rites were certainly not merely substitutionary methods of bearing penalties for sins. The Old Testament itself nowhere gives an explanation of these rites. To explain them three ideas have been tried: first, that of penal substitution, the sacrificial victim representatively bearing the guilt and punishment of the offerer; secondly, that of prayer generally, the sacrifices being symbolized expressions of diverse religious sentiments; thirdly, that of sacramental significance, the sacrifices being signs of spiritual realities and seals of spiritual blessings. It is not possible to enter into an extended examination of these sacrifices here. But we believe that a broad investigation will show that the first idea is too narrow, not agreeing, for instance, with the thank-offering, and especially not agreeing with the circumstance, which Davidson emphasizes, that the sacrificial system is conceived as being perpetuated in the restoration of God's kingdom as pictured by Ezekiel. The second idea is too vague, nor does it agree with the character of the old covenant, which was not a symbolic, but a real fellowship with God. The third idea is nearest to the truth, especially if it is so conceived as to include the truth of the other two. The old covenant sacrifices were not symbolic expressions of religious feelings, but operative institutions of God, in which the religious life of the covenant people found actual exercise and expression. As exercises of such as were already in the communion of God, they expressed all the religious feelings toward God which belonged to the manifestation and maintenance of this communion, prayer, adoration, gratitude, repentance and confession. But God also acted in them. As means of God's appointment, they were pledges of God's choice of his people and seals of His love and mercy towards them. The sacrifice involved a reciprocal relation between God and His people.

In the forward look to the atonement of Christ there are two points of special importance in the ritual of these sacrifices: the imposition of hands and the use of blood. The imposition of the hands of the offerer upon the victim evidently implies some kind of substitution, but not necessarily the transfer of sins, for it was done in the peace offerings which were thank offerings. But in reference to atonement for sin, as in burnt and sin offerings, the imposition of hands must have expressed a substitution of the victim as the bearer of the sin. This principle is expressly declared in reference to the goat sent to Azazel at the annual atonement, Lev 16:21. Although the person is in the covenant, his sinful blemishes must be atoned for, so that the anger of God may not fall upon him. The only explanation of the use of blood in the Old Testament is that in Lev 17:11. The blood is the life. God gave it upon the altar to make atonement, because the blood makes atonement by reason of the life. So then the central thing in the offering was the application of the blood, not the death of the victim. If we take in the idea of substitution here, we perceive that atonement is made to God by presenting an innocent life instead of the guilty life of the offerer. But the death is not an indifferent circumstance. It was inseparable from the procuring of the blood. Hence the substitutionary undergoing of death entered into the atonement. If this conception can be found nowhere else in the Old Testament, it at least occurs prominently in the picture of the suffering Servant of God in Isaiah 53, who was wounded for our transgressions and whose soul was made an offering for sin.

We come now to extra-ritual atonement. Sins committed with a high hand, Num 15:30, could not be atoned by sacrifice. They put the offender out of the covenant. But instances of extra-ritual and extraordinary Kippur or atonement occur in the Old Testament, the most notable being that effected through the intercession of Moses after the breach of the covenant in the sin of the golden calf, Ex 32:30. In such cases no priest can atone; it is God Himself who atones. And the object atoned is the sin, not as in the ritual a person who is already accepted, but with blemishes that require to be covered. In extra-ritual atonement there is usually an outbreak of God's wrath and punishment before forgiveness is granted. This is the form of atonement found in the New Testament, but blended with features of the ritual atonement.

These principles predominate in the Old Testament teaching of atonement: it is from God; it is an averting of God's anger; sacrificial atonement is substitutionary.

ATONEMENT IN THE NEW TESTAMENT

In the person of Jesus Christ God Himself has made an atonement for human sin. The life and especially the death of Christ were a vicarious sacrifice, by which propitiation was made to God for the sins of men, and thereby a reconciliation was effected in which the peace of God is turned to sinful men.

Between the Old Testament and the testimony of Christ about Himself falls the remarkable declaration of John the Baptist: "Behold, the Lamb of God," Jn 1:29, applying the prediction of Isaiah 53 to Jesus. The added explanation, "Which beareth and taketh away the sin of the world," interprets the significance of the designation to be that of sacrificial propitiation.

Taking up the testimony of Jesus Himself as it is given in the Synoptists, His general interpretation of His mission as mediatorial reveals the basis for what He says of His life and death as atoning. Standing between God and man He brings to man the truth and salvation of God. This mediatorial position is manifested in the manner of His teaching, in His healings, in His forgiving of sin, in His seeking and saving the lost, in His claim of faith in Himself, and in His claim that in Himself alone is the knowlege of the Father, Mt 11:27. Out of this mediatorial consciousness springs what He says of His death, that God requires it with a divine "must," Mt 16:21; that the giving of His life is a ransom for many, by which they are released from their guilt before God, Mt 20:28; and that His blood is covenant blood, like that described in Ex 24:8, poured out for many unto remission of sins, Mt 26:28, hence a sacrificial offering to God to remove the guilt of men.

In the gospel of St. John Jesus' self-witness manifests the same mediatorial claim found in the Synoptists, only with a stronger assertion of His power and office to supply divine life to men dead in sin. The sacrificial character of His death receives full expression, Jn 3:14; 10:15, and also His consecration of Himself as the atoning sacrifice by which His own are cleansed from all guilt, Jn 17:19.

The apostolic testimony only gives more definitely formulated statement to what Christ said of Himself. From the earliest to the latest of the New Testament books, from 1 Th 1:10: "Jesus delivered us from the wrath to come" to the doxology of the redeemed in Rev 5:12: "Worthy is the lamb that was slain, to receive power," etc., the underlying doctrine of all doctrines is the atonement by Christ's death. The prominence given to the story of Christ's passion in the four gospels confirms this.

St. Paul declares Christ crucified to be the substance of his gospel, 1 Co 1:23; 2:2. He does this because he finds there the ground of the justification of sinners, the divine possibility of the forgiveness of sins. The relation of sinful man to God was changed through the mediation of Christ. Sinners were transferred from under the wrath of God, Ro 1:18, into the state of God's peace, Eph 2:13, 14. The death of Christ was a sacrifice to God, Eph 5:2, propitiatory, Ro 3:25, vicarious, Ro 5:6, 8; 2 Co 5:14, on account of our sins, Ro 4:25, a substitutionary bearing of our sins, 2 Co 5:21, and of our curse, Gal 3:13.

St. Peter also views the death of Christ as a sacrifice. The elect condition of believers is due to sprinkling of the blood of Christ, 1 Pet 1:2, that is, by the propitiation of their sins through the death of Christ. The blood of Christ, as of a lamb without blemish and without spot, like the passover sacrifice, is a means of redemption, 1 Pet 1:19. Christ's crucifixion was a sacrificial and vicarious bearing of our sins in His body on the tree, 1 Pet 2:24, so that His death was our death for sin and His stripes our healing.

The epistle to the Hebrews presents the life and death of Christ as a higher sacrifice after the analogy of the sacrifices of the Old Testament. Christ is both high priest and victim, our substitute who has obtained eternal redemption for us by the holy character of His person and by His obedience unto death. He partook of human nature, Heb 2:14, and was made in all things except sin like His brethren, so that He might become their high priest, 2:17, who learned obedience by the things which He suffered, 5:8, a priest after the power of an endless life, 7:10, who offered Himself to God by the shedding of His blood, 9:14, once for all in order to bear the sins of many, 9:28, thereby doing the will of God as it referred to Him, 10:9, and effecting for us a sanctification from sin, that is, a freeing us from guilt before God 10:10. The stress laid upon obedience in this epistle is noteworthy. It is obedience to the particular will and appointment of God concerning Him that is meant. His death is the crowning act of His obedience. Not the suffering of Christ as pain, but the suffering as obedience makes His death a sacrifice, which is an adequate atonement for the sins of all. Cf. 10:5-10.

St. John's conception of Christ is dominated by the thought that He is the propitiation for our sins, 1 Jn 2:2; 4:10. Thereby He is the savior of the world, 4:14.

THE ATONEMENT AS PROPITIATION

The atonement of Christ is the means of averting the wrath of God. His obedience, both active and passive, is a propitiation, by which the sins of men are expiated before God and the reaction of God's holiness against sin is satisfied.

The conception of wrath in God is distasteful to many minds. But it is undoubtedly scriptural. And it is a necessary element in a perfect moral character. For there would be something wanting in goodness that would not react against evil. God's anger is the reaction of His holiness, the energetic assertion of His moral nature against sin. To this wrath we are subject on account of our sin, Jn 3:36; Ro 1:18; 5:9; Eph 2:3. For expressions of it by Jesus, although He does not use the word, compare Mt 10:28; Jn 8:24. Cf. also Heb 10:31; 12:29. On account of sin we are subject to the enmity of God, for, as the New Testament knows of an enmity of men towards God, it also knows of an enmity of God against men, as is evident from Ro 5:10; 11:28; Eph 2:16.

In this wrath and enmity of God on account of sin lies the necessity of a propitiation, that is, a means to avert the anger of God. What Christ presented to God in His holy life and death is called a propitiation in the New Testament, Ro 3:25; 1 Jn 2:2; 4:10; Heb 2:17. This correlation of God's wrath and Christ's propitiation shows that those explanations of the atonement, commonly called moral influence theories, are not in harmony with New Testament conceptions.

Christ's work undoubtedly has an influence upon human minds, bringing to bear motives and inducements to forsake sin and to seek after God. But this idea does not exhaust the truth of His atonement, nor is it the primary idea. As the subjective influence of prayer is real, but far from exhausting the idea of prayer, so the primary effect of the atonement is not on men, but on God. As a propitiation, it is the basis of a new line of action on the part of God.

What Christ rendered as the propitiation for the sins of the world comes out most manifestly in His death. Therefore that is often mentioned alone as if it were all. But His death was but the crowning exhibition of His obedience in doing God's will in bearing the sins of men. What preceded in His life was also propitiatory. Therefore it is correctly said that Christ made atonement by His active and His passive obedience. Nor must these be mechanically separated, as if His keeping the law in His conduct were only active, and His death only passive. In both His life and death He was always actively and passively obedient.

Christ rendered to God an expiation for our sins. But this expiation is not to be judged by the rule of an eye for an eye, a tooth for a tooth. It was a satisfaction of the reaction of God's holiness against sin, but not quantitatively considered. It is useless to try to measure the amount or degree of Christ's agony in His passion, and to ascribe to Him the enduring torments of hell in some sense. The satisfaction of the divine reaction against sin must be found in the character of His person and of His obedience, not in the pain of His sufferings as such.

THE ATONEMENT AS RECONCILIATION

The propitiation of Christ effected a reconciliation which proceeds from God to man, turns to the sinner the peace of God, and restores him to free access to God and communion with Him.

The reconciliation is God's gift, not man's task. Christ obtained it; man cannot make it. It is the offer of free divine grace, not the conciliating of God by man's attitude or conduct. The Bible speaks of God reconciling men, not of being reconciled. Argument is sometimes derived from this circumstance for the view that the effect of the atonement of Christ is only towards man and not towards God. It is denied that God needed to be reconciled by Christ. But this is a mistake, resting upon a misunderstanding of biblical idiom. In New Testament usage, quite contrary to our usage, the person giving the offense is said to be reconciled. Cf Mt 5:24. Accordingly when St. Paul says, "While we were enemies, we were reconciled to God through the death of His Son," Rom 5:10, he means that by the death of Christ that was done which made it possible for the favor and peace of God to be turned to us, or, as we would say, God was reconciled by Christ. The reconciliation is not something which we have in any way brought about, but as the apostle says, something which we have received, Rom 5:11. When St. Paul says, "God reconciled us to Himself through Christ," and "God was in Christ reconciling the world unto Himself," he adds the explanation, which shows that God's attitude towards sinners became different in view of the sacrifice of Christ: "Not reckoning unto them their trespasses," 2 Co 5 :18, 19. When the appeal is made to men, "Be reconciled to God," it is on the ground that the reconciliation has already been objectively accomplished through the vicarious suffering of the penalty of sin by Christ: "Him who knew no sin He made to be sin on our behalf," 2 Co 5:20, 21. The reconciliation was made when Christ in one body, namely His own, through the cross slew the enmity and became our peace, Eph 2:16. This reconciliation and peace we make our own by faith. "Being justified by faith, we have peace with God through our Lord Jesus Christ, through whom also we have had our access by faith into this grace wherein we stand." Ro 5:1-2.

THE ATONEMENT AS A VICARIOUS SATISFACTION

What has been done by Christ for man's salvation may be correctly conceived as a legal satisfaction, in which the God-man by His life and death rendered to divine justice in our stead full satisfaction for all our sins, which satisfaction sinful man could never make for himself and which Christ was able to make by reason of the divine dignity of His person and the consequent worth of His deeds and passion.

The Bible does not use the term satisfaction for the atonement of Christ. Indeed the form of its conceptions in regard to it is not that of civil law, but of religious law; it is not juridical, but sacrificial. However, it was very natural that legal conceptions should be used in the Church to explain the atonement. Christ Himself spoke of sins as debts. The New Testament idea of a price by which souls were purchased, easily passed over from the sacrificial to the civil form of conception. Legal ideas soon became current in the Church, even the idea of a satisfaction, although this idea was never applied to the atonement in the early Church. It was a legal conception when for a long time the death of Christ was regarded as a price paid to the devil as an equivalent for the souls of men. It was a legal line of thought when theological opinion divided on the question whether the death of Christ

was a price paid to the devil or to God. But it was not until
Anselm of Canterbury, at the end of the eleventh century,
philosophically formulated the doctrine that the price was
paid to God, that the conception of satisfaction became
dominant in the Church to explain the atonement.

Anselm's doctrine is in brief this: God has been
offended by sin—an infinite offence. To reestablish God's
honor an equivalent satisfaction was necessary. Only a divine
person could render this, for men, especially sinful men, were
not sufficient to cancel infinite guilt. Still the satisfaction had
to be rendered by man. So the Son of God became man and
became man's substitute. The voluntary sacrifice of the God-
man is an equivalent satisfaction for all sins.

The essential features of this doctrine became regnant
in the Church in the Middle Ages and were adopted by the
Reformers, and so it became orthodox in the great Protestant
Churches. It is found in the Lutheran confessions of faith,
although no special article treats of the atonement exclusively.
Objection is often made to the legal form of the doctrine of
vicarious satisfaction, because it obscures the ethical features
of the atonement. But the objection is not valid. The form is
not essential. All the essential elements of the biblical
doctrine of the atonement appear in the theory of vicarious
satisfaction. This shows itself clearly when it receives
devotional expression, as in the order for Communion in the
Lutheran Common Service:

> Our Lord Jesus Christ hath had mercy upon us, and
> hath taken upon Himself our nature, that so He might
> fulfill for us the whole will and law of God, and for us
> and for our deliverance suffer death and all that we by
> our sins have deserved.

THE EXALTATION OF CHRIST AND REDEMPTION

The reality of the forgiveness of sins and of deliverance from the power of sin and death is guaranteed to the believer in Christ by the exaltation of the Lord after His death, to wit, by His descent into Hades, His resurrection, His ascension, and His seat at the right hand of God.

Dogmatic tradition is wont to arrange the mediatorial work of Christ under three offices: priestly, prophetic and kingly. If we were following this arrangement we would give this section the title, The Kingly Office. But that arrangement appears to us more formal than logical. We do not question the truth that our Lord was prophet, priest and king, and that Old Testament prophecy represents the Messiah as fulfilling all that these three dignities of the theocratic kingdom embrace. But Christ was not prophet, priest and king successively in the fulfillment of His mediatorial office. He was always all of these in all His work. Therefore discarding this time-honored arrangement and looking at the real facts before us, we observe that after the atoning death of Christ the gospel tells of a series of great facts in the continued life of Christ, and we are led to inquire what bearing these have on our redemption. So the subject of this section is the bearing of the exaltation upon our redemption.

The first of these facts in the order of time is the descent of Christ into Hades. This must not be identified with Jesus being in the state of death for three days, of which the New Testament has little to tell. Christ alluded to it predictively, Mt 12:40, Lu 23:43, and St. Peter narratively as the background of the resurrection, Act 2:24sq. But what is technically called the descent into Hades or Hell, as the

Apostles' Creed has it, is something different. The passage, 1 Pet 3:19, "He went and preached unto the spirits in prison," comes into consideration here. The exegesis of this passage is much disputed. The vital question is what kind of preaching is meant here. Many think a preaching of salvation in the other world. Some Lutheran theologians, among them the famous John Gerhard, refer it to preaching through Noah upon earth. Most Lutheran theologians, correctly we believe, conceive of it as a preaching by Christ before His resurrection to the lost spirits in hell. The character of the preaching can only be inferred from the circumstances indicated in the context. As the subjects are characterized as those who abused the long-suffering of God, not an announcement of salvation but of the confirmation of their condemnation is accordant. The passage Col 2:15 is not a parallel, for the triumph described there is expressly declared to have been enacted on the cross. But there is an idea in Eph 4:9 which harmonizes with the conception of a triumphant descent of Christ into the hell of lost spirits. St. Paul specifies as a part of Christ's great achievement of filling all things that He descended into the lower parts of the earth. Lutheran orthodox dogmatics worked out the details of this obscure event in this form. On the morning of the resurrection Christ, after His revivification but before He showed Himself on earth, descended into hell and triumphantly manifested His victory over death and hell to devils and lost souls. This occurred in what to us is a very short interval of time. But in the other world time considerations do not hold. The moments of Easter morning between Christ's revivification and His manifestation on earth were fixed upon in order to maintain that Christ descended *tota persona*, in His whole person, hence with His body also.

It is wise not to try to define the details of the descent too accurately, as the Formula of Concord admonishes. That confession limits its doctrine to these essentials: Christ descended into hell in His whole person; He did so after His burial; by it He overcame the power of hell and despoiled the devil of his power.

The bearing of this mysterious transaction upon our salvation is this. We know, and the lost spirits know, that death and Satan cannot harm or pluck out of Christ's hand His redeemed.

The second great fact in Christ's exaltation is His resurrection. Negative criticism has in vain tried to explain this fact away. The identity of Christ's body is proved by the recognition of Him by the disciples after the resurrection, and by the empty grave. His body was visible and tangible, yet it was glorified, Phil 3:21, that is, it was not subject to material limitations, but was completely under the control and will of the spirit within.

The significance of the resurrection of Christ for our redemption is threefold. First, it marked the elevation of Christ to that form of existence which enables Him to provide by His personal presence and operation for the appropriation of the salvation which he purchased by His atonement. Cf. Mt 28:20. Secondly, it is a proof of perfected atonement. It is the divine evidence that the death of Christ was not an ordinary human death, but the means of our reconciliation with God. The claims of Jesus are vindicated by it, Rom 1:4. It is the ground of certainty that faith in Christ is not in vain, 1 Co 15:17. "He was delivered up for our trespasses, and was raised for our justification." Ro 4:25. The assurance of our justification by the death of Christ is given in His resurrection. Thirdly, the resurrection of Christ is the pledge and potency of the resurrection of those who believe in Him, Rom 8:11.

The resurrection cannot be separated from the forty days which followed, days in which the Lord appeared to His disciples to give to them their final preparation for their apostolic office, their completed knowledge of the Gospel, and their apostolic commission with the earnest and promise of their endowment with the Holy Spirit, Lu 24:47; Mt 28:19; Jn 20:22.

The third of the great facts of the exaltation of Christ is His ascension to heaven. The ascension has not its chief importance as an isolated event. This is true also of the resurrection. Both are proofs of the glorification of Christ, which the Lord claimed for Himself before His death, Jn 13:31; 17:1, and of which the transfiguration was the anticipation, Mt 17:1sq; 2 Pet 1:17. Jesus predicted His ascension, Jn 6:62; 20:17. The event, which is described in Mk 16:19; Lu 24:50; Act 1:9sq, is repeatedly referred to in the epistles as the token of His heavenly power and working in the Church, Eph 4:8; 1 Tim 3:16; 1 Pet 3:22; Heb 9:24. The heaven to which Christ ascended cannot be spatially conceived. Lutheran theology has always insisted on this in opposition to the Reformed idea of the circumscriptive locality of Christ in heaven. But Christ has His definite presence in heaven, however illocal it is, even as angels have their definite presence although they are pure spirits. Therefore the Lord's ascension was an actual local transference from the earth, not a mere disappearance, but it terminated in an illocal mode of presence in the heaven which is above all space.

The bearing of the ascension of Christ on our redemption lies in its connection with His enthronement in glory and the exercise of His unlimited power from on high for the salvation of the world.

The fourth fact in the exaltation of Christ, the sitting at the right hand of God, is not strictly an event, but a condition of existence. The phrase, the right hand of God, is obviously figurative. It expresses the possession of majesty and kingly power. On the basis of Ps 110:1 it is frequently applied to Christ in the New Testament. Cf Mt 22:44; Act 2:34; Ro 8:34, etc. The right hand of God is everywhere. This dictum of Luther became regulative in Lutheran theology to express the doctrine of the communication of divine majesty and power to the human nature of Christ, and was used to oppose the Reformed doctrine of the limited locality and power of the human nature of Christ in heaven.

The sitting of Christ at the right hand of the Majesty on high has this significance for our redemption. The gracious and omnipotent rule of Christ secures the welfare of His own in time and eternity and the extension of His kingdom unto its appointed end. This gracious rule Christ exercises as our prophet, priest and king. His prophetic office is continued in the ministry of His word in the Church, which He governs with the power of the Holy Spirit whom He sends, Eph 4:8 ; Jn 20:22. As priest He makes intercession for His own in heaven. As king He is the Head of the Church, to whom all powers in the world are subservient in the fulfilment of God's gracious purpose of salvation. Cf. Col 1:16-18; Eph 1:20-23; 1 Co 15:27; Heb 2:8.

The intercession of Christ requires a special remark. Christ made intercession for His disciples before His death. So the prayer in John 17 is called the high priestly prayer. His intercession in His heavenly exaltation is based upon His priestly atonement, Rom 8:34; Heb 7:25; 9:24; 1 Jn 2:1. We can form no idea of how this intercession is made within the internal relations of the Trinity. But for us the intercession means the continued application of the redemption for all needed blessings. Therefore Christian prayer is based on the intercession of Christ.

THE KINGDOM OF CHRIST AND THE KINGDOM OF GOD

The entire activity of Christ in His exaltation may be viewed as the exercise of His kingly office; for it is the exercise of His power and majesty in order to appropriate to mankind the fruits of His redemption, in grace upon earth and in glory in heaven. This kingly administration of the exalted Christ must be subsumed under the general idea of the kingdom of God.

We have now reached the point of transition from the objective realization of redemption by Christ to its personal application to men by the Holy Spirit. The connecting link between these two operations is the kingly reign of Christ in heaven.

The usual division of the kingly rule of Christ into the kingdom of grace, of power, and of glory is useful for practical purposes, but it should not create the impression that there are different departments of Christ's reign. It is all grace, glory and power. Christ was king while He was upon earth. As He said, for this was He born, Jn 18:37. But the full exercise of His kingship began after His ascension. The kingly office of Christ is not identical with the absolute sovereignty of God, in which of course the second person of the Trinity shares. It is an office of the incarnate Christ and especially consists in the elevation of His humanity to divine power and glory. It is a mediatorial office, pertaining to the work of redemption, and is the use of his power for the purposes of His grace. Since the world is subject to Him in the execution of His operation of redemption, it is a kingdom of power; and since the saints enjoy the fruits of His grace in glory, it is a kingdom of glory. The eschatological results of redemption are inseparable from the conception of the kingly reign of Christ. It works towards completed redemption and renewal of the world. There it reaches an end. It is a divine operation impelling and directing the history of the world to its divinely appointed consummation. The conclusion is marked by the final judgment. As has been remarked, it is not identical with God's omnipotent rule of the universe. The kingly redemptive reign of Christ is for a limited period, as St. Paul indicates in 1 Co 15:28. When the whole purpose of redemption shall have been perfected and the last enemy, death, shall have been abolished, "the Son Himself shall be subjected to Him, that did subject all things unto Him, that God may be all in all." This subjection of Christ to the Father does not mean a deposition or abdication, but the conclusion of redemption. After that the reign of Christ will be merged into the universal divine sovereignty. The Redeemer will participate in the eternal glory and majesty of God forever.

Christ's mediatorial kingly reign is an operation to bring in the kingdom of God. Therefore it must be subsumed under the general idea of the kingdom. What is the kingdom of God? The phrase has been thrown forward into great prominence in recent theological discussions. Jesus certainly put the kingdom of God in the foreground of His teaching. Whatever else He meant by the phrase, He at least meant that new order of things which was to set in with His coming. There is a remarkable infrequency of the term in the epistles, the word church being used, not as an equivalent but as a counterpart. But it, or its equivalent, the kingdom of heaven, occurs with very great frequency in the synoptists and sometimes also in the gospel of John. The kingdom of God, which Jesus announced to be at hand with His own coming, has its historical foundation in the Old Testament. The old covenant with its priestly, prophetic and kingly institutions was a preparatory realization of it. The divine kingdom was not identical with the Jewish political state. But the inward divine potency, which was manifested in the religious life of the Old Testament and its outward authorized forms, was the essence of the kingdom. It has its social side, but it is not merely an order of human society. The social bond in it is spiritual. When the Jewish state fell it did not perish. Christ did not connect it with any organization. It is not humanity living for moral purposes and ideals, as many in recent years have conceived. Christ laid down moral conditions of entrance into it, and declared the exclusion of the Jews of His day from it on account of moral unfitness. But moral life is not the kingdom, but the fruit of the kingdom. The kingdom is a gift of God, Mt 21:43. Its coming is to be sought from God by prayer, as Jesus taught in the model prayer. Jesus illustrated its characteristics in various parables, which show that it is a divine creation, and that it has growth and progress. It is a present fact, Lu 17:21, and yet is frequently spoken of as a thing to come. Its full manifestation is dependent upon Christ's redemptive activity. What then is it? It is the rule of God, the rule of the moral and spiritual in fullness and perfection. It is the rule of God that is attended with that blessed condition of man and human society that salvation brings to pass, beginning with conversion to God, progressing through the Church, ending with the coming of

Christ and the consummation of perfection, in which mankind shall be free from sin and death, the world sanctified and glorified, and God's will perfectly done.

Chapter VIII
THE HOLY SPIRIT
The Application of Redemption by the Holy Spirit in the Church Through the Means of Grace

THE OFFICE OF THE HOLY SPIRIT

The personal application and appropriation of the redemption that was effected by Christ to sinful man are necessary to make that redemption efficacious for deliverance from sin and its consequences. This is the office of the Holy Spirit.

That part of theology which treats of the Holy Spirit is technically called pneumatology. The personality and divinity of the Spirit have already been discussed under the head of the Trinity. Here the office of the Holy Spirit in the plan of redemption is taken up.

It is important to realize that the Holy Spirit has a distinct redemptive office. His operation is not a general circumambient influence. In the historical revelation of God the Holy Spirit comes distinctively into the foreground at a certain stage. As the Son of God had a mission and was sent, so also the Holy Spirit has a mission in the world and is sent. Jn 14:26; 15:26; 16:7. His mission had a historical beginning. "The Spirit was not yet (given); because Jesus was not yet glorified," Jn 7:39. Surely the Spirit was not previously absent from the world. The whole Old Testament shows that. But after the coming of Christ the Spirit was present in a different way. He is present to apply the grace of God manifested in Christ. In view of the special manifestations of the presence and working of the Spirit in the age of the apostles, that age may suitably be called the age of the Spirit. That period is fundamental and normal for the Church in all subsequent time. For this reason the Scriptures produced in it under the special operation of the Holy Spirit are of unique character and value.

But in a wider sense the age of the Spirit still continues. The salvation from sin, which was brought into the world by Christ, is wrought into the lives of men as a subjective possession by the Holy Spirit. This appropriation of salvation comes from the Lord enthroned in regal glory, for the Spirit is sent by Christ. Hence the Spirit is called the Spirit of Christ, Rom 8:9; Phil 1:19; 1 Pet 1:11; Gal 4:6, and the experience of the working of the Spirit of Christ in us is identical with that of Christ in us, Rom 8:9-10. The Spirit is the Giver of Life, Jn 6:63; 2 Co 3:6. A study of the numerous passages in the New Testament which speak of the Holy Spirit will show that the manifold grace of God, purchased and won for us by Christ, is communicated in vital efficacy by the Holy Spirit. Hence as the gift that includes all spiritual gifts, the Holy Spirit is the chief gift of God, Lu 11:13; Rom 5:5.

THE HOLY SPIRIT AND THE HOLY SCRIPTURES

The saving activity of the Holy Spirit is exercised in the use of the Word of God. This Word of God exists now in its fundamental form in the Holy Scriptures. The spiritual effects, which are produced by the instrumentality of the Holy Scriptures, are due to their character as the inspired Word of God. The adaptedness of the Scriptures to be the divinely given means for the gracious operations of the Holy Spirit is expressed in certain attributes, among which four are especially important: authority, clearness, efficacy and sufficiency.

Neither experience nor scriptural evidence justifies the idea that the Holy Spirit works faith and spiritual effects by a direct and unmediated illapse upon the soul. Neither experience nor scriptural evidence certifies to any action of the Holy Spirit that establishes saving relations of the soul to Christ apart from the Word of God. In short, nobody ever became a Christian without the Word of God in some form. The study of the work of the Holy Spirit therefore leads to the study of that Word, which He uses as the means of His gracious operations.

The Word of God that brings to man the revelation of God is a body of truth which has been given by God historically. It is deposited in the Bible. The same truth declared in the Church in harmony with the teaching of Scripture is also the Word of God. But the fundamental and normative form of the Word of God is that of the Holy Scriptures.

It was for a long time traditional in dogmatic method to treat of the Holy Scriptures at the beginning before all other doctrines. We prefer to treat of the doctrine of the Scriptures here chiefly because we believe their unique character can be best understood from their function as the means for the gracious operations of the Holy Spirit.

We get at the idea of the Christian Scriptures historically. The origin of the writings of the New Testament in the apostolic age imparts to them a distinctive significance, for that was the age of the foundation-laying, normative activity of the Holy Spirit. It was the pentecostal age. Hence the writings produced in the apostolic circle in that age are normative for the Church. The Old Testament Scriptures were recognized by the apostles and by Christ Himself as normative, and accordingly they are normative for the Church.

The Holy Scriptures are the Word of God. Whatever was the original form in which God revealed God Himself to men, whether by prophets or apostles or in Christ, we have the revelation now only in the record of it contained in the Scriptures. The fact that the Holy Scriptures are a record must not lead to the idea that they are only historical documents, from which the Word of God must be extracted by some test which man has in himself. The phrase, correct in itself, that the Scriptures contain the Word of God, has been put to such a perverted use. By it a distinction has been made between what is and what is not the Word of God in the Scriptures, a distinction like kernel and shell. But the Bible is the Word of God. For by the Word of God must not be understood certain ideas apart from the language which is their expression. God's truth has historically received expression in the writings of the Bible. That expression is now the Word of God. The human form of expression found in the Bible sometimes causes erroneous thoughts here. The vital point is not the form of expression. However elegant or inelegant, perfect or imperfect, precise or inaccurate the language of the Bible may be, God's truth of salvation is expressed authoritatively in the Scriptures.

This is the normative Word of God because it is inspired. The Scriptures were written by men, yet they are the Word of God. This is explained by the fact of inspiration. It needs to be particularly noted that inspiration, as the word is used in theology, refers to the production of the books of the Bible. The statement sometimes made, that not the books but the men were inspired, is fallacious. Apostles and prophets were indeed inspired men. But the inspiration in connection with the Bible refers to a certain action of God in the production of the writings it contains.

To define that action is difficult, for we have no personal experience of it. Its nature must be inferred from the facts presented in the Bible. The construction of a theory of inspiration by a priori deduction is vicious. Such a priori reasoning from a theoretical idea to the facts in the case is a fault of the old mechanical theory of inspiration, which is so little satisfying, and in turning away from which many in recent times have departed from the truth of inspiration itself. There are two orders of facts that must receive due consideration in forming an idea of what inspiration is. First are those facts about the Bible which pertain to the truth that God speaks through the Scriptures. Secondly, there are the facts that pertain to the production of these writings by men with human limitations and personal characteristics. The first class of facts includes prophetic utterances, the language of Christ, His promise of the Spirit to guide His disciples, the claim of apostles to speak the Word of God, and the citation of Old Testament language in the New Testament as God's Word. The second class of facts includes all that pertains to the literary composition of the books of the Bible and to the historical progress of revelation. It is unnecessary to enter into details. But a remark is necessary in regard to human limitations and fallibility. We have no dogmatic right or reason to decide before critical examination of the facts that human limitations were miraculously overcome and the possibility of human errancy was absolutely removed by the Holy Spirit. The evidence contained in the Bible must decide that. This statement is made to free the doctrine of inspiration from the encumbrance of a priori assumptions, like the old argument that the Hebrew vowel points must have been in the original Scriptures and inspired, and like the abstraction that the original autographs were faultless.

From these two classes of facts it is evident that in the Bible divinely given material and human elaboration are combined. The dogmatic question of inspiration then is this: How was the divine content combined with the human presentation?

Theories of inspiration (where real inspiration and not a state of mind like poetic inspiration is thought of) have been divided into two groups: mechanical and dynamic. In the mechanical theory inspiration is conceived like dictation to an amanuensis. In the dynamic view the powers of the writer are conceived as acting freely, but are heightened by the power of the Holy Spirit operating upon them in the natural act of writing. The dynamic view accords best with the facts presented in the Bible.

The doctrine of verbal inspiration is often confused with the mechanical dictation theory of inspiration. But inspiration may extend to the language and be verbal without dictation. A dynamic theory of inspiration may also be verbal. Every page of the Bible proves that the action of the writers was like the action of other men who write. But Christian faith recognizes that in this process of composition and writing the mind of the Spirit found expression through the words written, even where the same thing was given in variant forms, as frequently occurs in the gospels. The Spirit dynamically cooperated in the writing, not as an author behind the author, but as God works in and through men, heightening, purifying, directing conceptions and expressions. Without adopting any such mechanical view of verbal inspiration as the old orthodoxy maintained, we hold to the essential truth of the leading positions which it sought to defend: from the Holy Spirit came the suggestion of the matter, the suggestion of the words, and the impulse to write. But suggestion is not to be identified with dictation nor impulse with mechanical motion.

The principal scriptural proof of inspiration is the Bible itself. But certain texts indicate how the writers of the New Testament realized that the mind of the Spirit was expressed in what was written by others or uttered by themselves. Cf. 2 Tim 3:16; 1 Pet 1:11; 2 Pet 1:21; 1 Co 2:13; 1 Th 2:13.

Four attributes of the Bible mark its adaptedness to be the instrument of the gracious operations of the Holy Spirit: authority, perspicuity, sufficiency and efficacy. The emphasizing of these four attributes is due to the controversy between Protestants and Roman Catholics in regard to the Scriptures as the source and rule of faith.

The truth of God as set forth in the Scriptures is the only test of Christian teaching, and all differences in regard to doctrine must be finally decided by the Bible. This is called normative authority. Moreover, the truth of God is so set forth in the Scriptures that by them faith is produced and the mind of man is subjected to their teaching. This is called causative authority. Hence the authority of the Scriptures is of two kinds.

The Scriptures are self-explanatory. There are obscurities in the Bible, but the Scriptures interpret themselves, so that no external tribunal of interpretation, such as the Roman Church with its papal authority claims to be, is admissible. This is the scriptural attribute of perspicuity or clearness.

The saving truth of God is fully set forth in the Bible. No additional source of divine truth, such as the Roman and

Greek Churches claim to possess in tradition, or such as the judgments of natural reason, can be allowed. This is the scriptural attribute of sufficiency.

The truth of God in the Bible as such works conviction. As inspired writings the Scriptures have inherent power to produce faith and godliness. The Scriptures have the attribute of efficacy.

SAVING GRACE

The active favor of God, by which a sinful man is made a participant in the redemption of Christ, is called grace. Since the grace of God in Christ is imparted by the Holy Spirit, it is called the grace of the Holy Spirit. By its very nature as free favor and gratuitous blessing of God, grace excludes all merit of man in salvation. The natural will and powers of man are in no sense or degree a cause of salvation.

The Greek word for grace is one of that class of words which, as Trench says, "taken up into Christian use are glorified and transformed." Its general meaning is favor. Specifically it is used of God's favor with respect to sin. Contrasting it with mercy, Bengel tersely and instructively says: "Grace removes guilt, mercy misery." The grace of God is an active principle.

> It is used of the merciful kindness by which God, exerting His holy influence upon souls, turns them to Christ, keeps, strengthens, increases them in Christian faith, knowledge, affection, and kindles them to the exercise of the Christian virtues.[4]

---

[4] Cf. Thayer's Lexicon of the N. T.

In the New Testament the word belongs especially to the Pauline vocabulary. From meaning God's disposition of favor the word passes over to the idea of His effective working in Christ, and then to the blessings received by the individual from this working. Therefore saving grace is the active favor of God in Christ, by which the blessings of salvation are appropriated to sinful man.

In theology it is customary to speak of the grace of the Holy Spirit. The New Testament never uses this phrase. It speaks of the grace of God, or of Christ. However, as the effects of grace are ascribed to the Holy Spirit in the New Testament, the expression is justified. It is a convenient, comprehensive designation.

In Augustine the word grace took on the idea of communicated power, which is a deflection of its biblical meaning. Among the scholastics of the Middle Ages this conception of communicated power was construed as a quality infused into the soul, a notion which opened the door for the doctrine of human merit in salvation. Grace is not something infused, a transforming quality put into the nature of man. Grace does not act upon man as a substance receives impressions. It acts upon him as a personality. It is an active principle, the manifestation of divine energy exerted by the Holy Spirit; but its action is not physical, but spiritual and moral. Its primary effect is not moral transformation, but forgiveness of sins, that is, a new relation to God, out of which arises a new moral life.

To define the relation of divine grace to the human will has always been a difficult problem in the Church. The early Church, especially the Greek writers, emphasized the freedom of the will not withstanding the effects of sin. Hence they conceived conversion as a cooperation of grace and the human will. In the great controversy between Augustine and Pelagius the extremes came into a decisive conflict. Pelagius, a stern moralist, magnified human freedom to the utmost. For him grace was hardly more than instruction. Augustine, with an overwhelming sense of the bondage of the will in sin and with a realistic conception of grace, pressed the doctrine of the monergism of the divine will to the extreme of determinism and the irresistibility of grace. A middle view, which was really the more ancient view, was advocated by John Cassian, the cooperation of grace and the human will in salvation. This is called Semipelagianism. Augustine's doctrine, somewhat tempered, became the official teaching of the Church; but Semipelagianism crept in more and more, especially in the centuries before the Reformation. The Reformers both in Germany and Switzerland returned to Augustinianism, but in the Lutheran Church the inference of irresistible grace was rejected. By a change of view on the part of Melanchthon, who taught a faculty of applying or adapting oneself to grace, a slight element of cooperation of man with grace was introduced into the doctrine of conversion, which the bitter synergistic controversies in the Lutheran Church raged over and which the Formula of Concord finally rejected.

The solution of this problem of the relation of the human will to God's grace must be found within certain fixed limits. On the one hand, both the corruption of man's nature by sin, with the consequent bondage of the will, and salvation by grace alone exclude any cooperation of man's will in conversion. On the other hand, grace is not compulsion. It acts upon man as an intelligent moral personality. The connecting link must be found in the creative operation of grace. The Holy Spirit creates faith in the heart. This implies that He restores in some degree the freedom of the will in the act of conversion. The will contributes nothing to the salvation of man. It must first be renewed before the first motions to regenerate life can arise. But the will can resist the Holy Spirit and continue in sin.

Under the operation of divine grace man passes through successive spiritual experiences. Accordingly theologians make a formal distinction between grace prevenient to conversion, operating in conversion, cooperating after conversion, and persevering to the end.

SAVING FAITH

Salvation through Christ is laid hold of by man in faith, which is the soul's attitude of trust towards God. In this trust man looks confidently for that righteousness, of which he knows himself to be in need, as the gift of God on account of the merits of Christ.

Faith is a central idea, on the human side the central idea in Christianity. The full conception of faith came with the full revelation of salvation in Christ. In the Old Testament the conception of faith is much less prominent than in the New. Indeed in one place St. Paul speaks of the time before Christ as the time when faith had not yet come, Gal 3:23. In the Old Testament faith is essentially Messianic, looking to the future. Cremer remarks: "Faith is spoken of in the Old Testament where the foundations of the New Testament are laid." It is trustful waiting for God, a form of expression much more frequently used than believing, Gen 15:6; Is 7:9; Hab 2:4. Cf. Ps 130:5; Is 40:31; Lam 3:26 ; Mic 7:7, etc.

In the New Testament use there is an intellectual element in faith, knowledge of what is revealed and assent to it. But the predominating element is trust. We observe that Jesus demanded faith as the sole condition of receiving His help and the blessing of God. In the gospel of John faith refers more particularly to the person of Christ, and the intellectual element is prominent. The complete development of the distinctively Christian idea of faith is found in St. Paul. By setting it in contrast with works, as a factor entirely to be excluded in obtaining righteousness from God, St. Paul brings out the element of confidence as the essential characteristic of faith. Cf. Ro 3:28; 4:5, 13; Gal 3:23-26; 5:4, 5. The description of faith in Heb 11:1 is not a definition in the dogmatic sense, but a description from the angle of future hope.

The Pauline idea of faith was soon obscured in the Church. Very soon the intellectual element of assent was made prominent. For Augustine faith was assent and obedience to the doctrines of the Church. So it remained in the Middle Ages, and so it is in the Roman Catholic Church yet. As ignorant persons could not know all the doctrines of the Church, an implicit faith was required. It was soon realized that this intellectual assent or historical faith could not save a man. It was therefore construed as the beginning of righteousness, which had to be completed in another form. This other form was love. Scholastic theology made a distinction between "*fides informis*" (mere assent) and "*fides formata*" (faith perfected by love). The latter then was made the real cause of salvation. The Reformation restored the New Testament conception of faith as trust, excluding love and works as grounds of salvation and making them fruits of faith in the justified man. The faith which the Reformers made central and decisive in Christian life and experience, is special, justifying faith, that is, faith in Christ. The Roman Catholic theologian, Bellarmine, has sharply but correctly drawn the distinction between the conception of faith in his Church and among Protestants, as follows: As to the object of justifying faith, Protestants restrict it to the promise of grace, Catholics include in it everything in the Word of God; as to the mental faculty, Protestants locate faith in the will, Catholics in the intellect; as to the act itself, Protestants define it as "*fiducia*" (trust), Catholics as "*assensus*" (assent).

In the scholastic development of Lutheran theology faith was analyzed into three constituents: knowledge, assent and trust. The analysis has been criticized in recent years as savoring of intellectualism. But the fault of intellectualism, where it occurs, lies not in the requirement of knowledge, but in the form in which the knowledge is demanded. Faith is intelligent trust, necessarily involving knowledge of the gospel and mental assent to it. How faith arises in the soul is, just like other states of the mind, a mystery that eludes perfect observation. Experience teaches that faith will not arise under every condition of the soul. Inseparable from it is that revulsion of the heart from sin that is called repentance. Logically repentance precedes faith, and yet it is true that real repentance before God, as distinct from mere remorse, requires faith. It is impossible to apply to our souls the redemption of Christ without applying to our lives the just judgment of God against sin. But conversely, the gravity of God's judgment against sin never becomes so clear as when we look upon Christ. Faith is a state of the mind and will, and yet it is not the product of the mind and will. It is God's work in a human soul. It is God's gift. To say that God gives the ability to believe does not express the full truth. The Holy

Spirit works faith, Jo 6:44; Phil 1:29; Eph 2:8. He works faith through the Word of God. "Belief cometh of hearing, and hearing by the Word of Christ," Ro 10:17. Cf. Gal 3:2, where the apostle argues that by the hearing or message of faith we receive the Spirit who creates our faith. The effect of faith in Christ is first a new relation to God, and then a new shaping of our thought and conduct. The new relation to God is justification, the forgiveness of our sins. Faith belongs to the moral life. It is a personal attitude of the soul. But it is not a moral work among other moral works. Its efficacy lies simply in its apprehensive quality. Nevertheless it is, as Luther said, a living, active thing. A new shaping of thought and conduct results from this soul-renewing trust. The correct relation of justifying faith to moral life is technically defined in the formula, "*Fides quae viva justificat*" (faith justifies and it is a living thing) in contrast to the erroneous formula, "*fides qua viva*" (faith inasfar as it is living justifies.) Faith saves not because of the life it produces, but because it is faith, that is, an apprehension of the Savior Christ.

Saving faith is belief of the heart. The word for faith in the Scriptures generally means this belief. But sometimes in the New Testament and frequently in other usage faith means that which is believed, the content of belief. Theologically this distinction is expressed in the two formulas: "*fides qua creditur*" (the faith of the heart) and "*fides quae creditur*" (the content of faith, the creed).

JUSTIFICATION

Correlative to saving faith in man is justification by God. Justification is a forensic act, that is, an act of divine judgment, by which God freely forgives a sinner his sins because He imputes to him the righteousness of

Christ. Therefore justification is a new relation of acceptance with God for Christ's sake. It is by faith alone, because faith apprehends Christ who by His obedience is righteousness for us before God.

In the Smalcald Articles Luther says of justification: "Of this article nothing can be yielded or conceded, though heaven and earth may fall." The whole conception of Christianity is determined by the conception which one has of justification.

To explain the scriptural teaching on justification it is necessary to note first the meaning of the word, and then its connection with faith. The precise meaning of the word justify in the Bible is of particular importance because much of the controversy between Protestantism and Romanism hinges upon the signification of the term. Roman Catholic theology contends for the meaning, to make just or righteous; Protestant theology for the meaning, to pronounce righteous. The Roman conception is that of a moral transformation, the Protestant conception that of a new relation, a judicial change. The Protestant contention is fully supported by the usage of both the Hebrew word for justify in the Old Testament and the Greek word in the New Testament. In both languages the biblical use of the word is legal, meaning to pronounce or evince righteous. It is used in connection with judicial transactions. Cf. Ex 23:7; Deut 25:1; 2 Sam 15:4; 1 Kg 8:32; Job 27:5; Is 5:23; 50:8; Mt 12:37; Act 13:39; Ro 2:13; Tit 3:7. The synonymous words are also forensic. Cf. Gen 15:6; Ps 32:2, etc. As the word especially belongs to the Pauline vocabulary, it is important to note that he speaks of reckoning righteousness to one, Ro 4:4, 5; 2 Co 5:19, 20, a use that cannot signify the imparting of a quality, but signifies a legal relation. Therefore to justify in biblical language means to show to be in the right, to pronounce righteous. In regard to man's relation to God it expresses a legal standing before God, an acceptance by God on terms which He approves.

The connection of faith with justification is everywhere assumed in the Old Testament, for the interpretation of all piety in the Old Testament in the eleventh chapter of Hebrews as an exhibition of faith is historically correct. The infrequent use of the word faith in the Old Testament, which made St. Paul cling to a few texts like Hab 2:4 and Gen 15:6, does not affect this statement. The idea of faith is abundantly expressed by other terms, notably by waiting for. In the New Testament faith is explicitly laid down everywhere as the condition of receiving God's blessings. Christ demanded it as the requirement to obtain healing, forgiveness and all divine blessings. Lu 7:47 ("Her sins, which are many, are forgiven; for she loved much") is not an exception. It declares that love is the proof that forgiveness has been received, not the condition on which it was received. The doctrine of justification by faith was worked out into formal statement especially by St. Paul in his contention with Jewish legalism. His doctrine is built upon four propositions. First, justification is by grace, Ro 4:16; Eph 2:8. Second, it is a judicial sentence of God based upon the work of Christ, Gal 3:13; Ro 3:24; 5:8-9; 1 Co 1:30. Third, it is by reckoning to the sinner righteousness on account of Christ's merits, 2 Co 5:21; Ro 4:5-6; 4:11; 5:19; Phil :9. Fourth, the condition of justification is faith, Ro 3:22; 4:11-13; 9:30; Gal 2:16; 3:8, 24. Faith is the condition of justification, not because it is a merit or a satisfaction rendered to God by a sinner, but because it apprehends the merits of Christ's atonement.

According to this biblical doctrine justification consists of two elements, which however are but two sides of one act of God: the forgiveness of sins, and the imputation of the righteousness of Christ to the sinner. It is an act of God in the forum of heaven, but it is experienced here by sinners in faith, by which they know that Christ has delivered them from condemnation and has brought them the reconciliation and peace of God, Ro 5:1.

The connection between this free, forensic justification and personal holiness of life may present some difficulty to the student. For if we are justified, as Luther was wont to say, by an "alien" righteousness, where are the springs of a new life? How does forgiveness of sins beget a new life? It is a standing objection of Roman Catholics that the Lutheran doctrine permits the believer to continue in sin. Now it is of some significance that St. Paul encountered the very same objection. "Shall we continue in sin that grace may abound?" Rom 6:1. The bonds of connection between justification and personal holiness are vital. First, faith itself as trust in God is a surrender of the sinner to God. It is the living, active thing, the spontaneous source of God-pleasing action, which Luther described so magnificently in his famous Preface to the epistle to the Romans. Secondly, faith manifests itself in gratitude towards God, as St. John says: "We love, because He first loved us. If God so loved us, we also ought to love one another." 1 Jn 4:11, 19. Thirdly, faith is a relation to God in which the Holy Spirit and Christ through Him dwell in the heart of the believer. This is the argument grandly developed by St. Paul in the eighth chapter of Romans and in Gal 5:16-25.

We are now prepared to look at the apparent contradiction of St. Paul's doctrine in the epistle of St. James. "If a man say he hath faith, but have not works, can that faith save him?" Ja 2:14. We do not know what form of error St.

James was opposing, but we do know that St. Paul himself
would have said that such faith would save no man. St. James
is speaking of a perversion of the word faith, of an unfruitful,
dead faith, such as demons also have, which is the very
contrary of the faith of Abraham, which God reckoned unto
Him for righteousness.

The revival of the scriptural doctrine of justification
by Luther was effected in opposition to the Roman Catholic
doctrine received from the scholastics. According to the latter
doctrine, later sanctioned as the doctrine of the Roman
Catholic Church at the Council of Trent, justification is a
process in man, by which inherent holiness is infused into
him and he is transformed from a sinner into a righteous
man. The beginning of the process is marked by faith, that is,
the intellectual acceptance of the doctrines of the Church.
This faith must receive an inward content, must be perfected
by love, which is the meritorious ground of justification. Here
comes in the feature of works-righteousness, that
characterizes this doctrine of justification. The Lutheran
doctrine has had to be defended against alterations of it,
which have been attempted at various times within the
Lutheran Church. For instance, in the age of the Reformation
Osiander taught justification by faith, but not as a forensic
act, but as a mystical infusion of the divine righteousness of
Christ into the sinner. This error was vigorously opposed by
Melanchthon and others and was finally dealt with in the
Formula of Concord. In the nineteenth century various
theologians have endeavored to introduce the moral change,
which faith in Christ produces, as a part of the ground of
justification, e.g., Beck and Hengstenberg. The Liberal
theology of the present day is much influenced by the
moralistic theology of Ritschl. The leading features of his

theory of justification are these. Justification is forgiveness of sins, which God grants freely. The death of Christ and His merits are not the ground of forgiveness. It is an absolutely free act of God's love. In His religious life Christ showed that God is love. From Him the sinner learns to give up his distrust of God and so advances from the consciousness of guilt to the consciousness of God's grace. That is his justification, which is then proved by his moral life in the fulfillment of his vocation, just as Christ fulfilled His vocation.

THE ORDER OF SALVATION

The justified person in the rise and progress of his spiritual life is always under the influence of the Holy Spirit. The various modifications in the gracious operation of the Holy Spirit, by which the salvation in Christ is applied to the believer, and the corresponding modifications in the inner life of the justified soul may be analyzed and arranged in a logical order. Such an arrangement is called the order of salvation.

Justification makes a sinner a child of God. It is that adoption of which the Scriptures speak, Eph 1:5; Rom 8:15, 23; Gal 4:5; 1 Jn 3:1. The Christian never gets beyond this. His whole life is lived in this relation of forgiveness for Christ's sake. There is a beginning, progress and perfecting of the life of faith, but all is in the state of justification and under the grace of the Holy Spirit imparted in it. Therefore justification is not to be included in the order of salvation, as has often been done in doctrinal treatises; it is the divine background and substratum of the life of faith.

The name Order of Salvation dates from the early part of the eighteenth century, but the arrangement designated by it is older. Having its roots in the new conception of Christianity centering in justification introduced by the Reformation, it was worked out by the theologians of the seventeenth century. Pietism made much use of it practically, sometimes with a tendency to divide the Christian life up into stages through which the soul was expected to pass in temporal succession. This destroys the unity of the grace of God in Christ imparted by the Holy Spirit. The order of salvation is logical, not temporal. While there has been a general agreement as to the order for several centuries, various differences appear in the treatment of the subject by Lutheran writers. The following order of Hollazius may be regarded as typical of older theology. The arrangement in a more recent book, entitled The Order of Salvation, by Emil Wacker, may serve as an example of a present-day arrangement. Hollazius arranges: Vocation, illumination, conversion, regeneration, justification, mystical union, renovation, preservation, glorification. Wacker arranges with reference to God's action and corresponding human experience: Vocation and awakening, illumination and spiritual knowledge, conversion and the outburst of repentance and faith, sealing and certainty of salvation, renovation and walk in a state of grace, preservation in the faith and Christian perseverance, perfecting in the faith and Christian perfection.

The Bible itself contains no such scheme of order of salvation. Wherever there is a seeming succession of operations of grace, as in 1 Co 1:30, 6:11, Tit 3:5-6, the fullness and not the order of divine grace is expressed. But the New Testament uses a variety of expressions to designate different aspects of the operative grace of God, and in the arrangement of an order of salvation these should be especially considered. But it should be remembered that these terms are not scientific, but generally figurative, and that they are descriptions of the same general spiritual fact from different points of view. This remark, by the way, applies to the language of Luther's Catechism in the explanation of the third article of the Creed. The words, "Called me by the Gospel" etc. are not properly an *Ordo Salutis*.

In distinguishing different operations of grace it is here instructive to view each both actively and passively, that is, as God's act and as an effect received by man. The fuller consideration of the latter side belongs to Ethics, which discusses the states of the soul in the progress of the Christian life. Underlying the consideration of the successive items in the order of salvation, in the paragraphs which follow, is this scheme of arrangement, according to the general conception of the rise, the progress, and the perfecting of the work of grace in the soul: 1. The rise: a) vocation and obedience of faith; b) illumination and knowledge of salvation; c) regeneration and consciousness of salvation; d) conversion and repentance with surrender to God. 2. The progress: a) sealing and certainty of salvation; b) sanctification and pursuit of holiness. 3. The perfecting: a) preservation and perseverance; b) perfecting and the Christian ideal.

VOCATION AND OBEDIENCE OF FAITH

Vocation is the act of the Holy Spirit by which through the Word of God He calls sinners to partake of the blessing of salvation in Christ. Its effect in the sinner is to awaken him to obedience of faith.

We have advisedly refrained from defining vocation as an invitation. It is not because we would deny that the Scriptures present the gospel offer of salvation in the light of an invitation. Mt 11:28 is the gracious invitation. In the parables of the Lord guests are invited. Is 55:1 is a free invitation. But the Gospel offer is not mere invitation. The Word of God is the means of the Spirit's working. Accordingly the conception of the biblical words call, calling and called, is not simply that of invitation, but efficacious invitation. Vocation, as the Bible speaks of it, implies the communication of the grace to obey the invitation. The subject is God. He calls and His call presents the ground of a real, personal relation to Himself. Therefore St. Paul says: "Faithful is He that calleth you, who will also do it," 1 Th 5:24. But the effect of the call is not always the same, although a man who has been called is never the same thereafter. The apostle says: "We are a sweet savor of Christ unto God, in them that are being saved, and in them that are perishing; to the one a savor from death unto death; to the other a savor from life unto life," 2 Co 2:15-16. In the epistles the "called" are members of the Church, never those who refuse the call. Hence there is no practical difference between the "called" and the "elect." In the use of the word all stress is laid on the divine efficiency. Vocation is the application of the efficacious Word of God, 1 Th 2:12-13; 2 Th 2:14.

Lutheran theology teaches that the call of God is serious and efficacious in all, but is resistible, hence not always effectual. Cf. Mt 23:37. "Ye would not." Absolute predestinarians logically hold that God's call is irresistible, hence efficacious only in the elect. As God's gracious purpose of salvation in Christ is universal, vocation is in principle universal, although we are unable to tell how it is universally realized.

The effect of God's call in the human heart is the obedience of faith. The inward experience of God's vocation is faith, a yielding of the person to the gracious will of God for salvation. Faith, which is trust, is also obedience, not obedience to God's commands (although this follows), but obedience to His promises. In this sense the New Testament speaks of obedience of faith and obeying the faith, Rom 1 :5; 16 :26; Act 6:7, as it speaks of obeying the truth or the gospel, 1 Pet 1:22; Ro 10:16. To believe obediently to the Word of God that we have been redeemed by Christ from sin and death, this is to live in the vocation of God.

ILLUMINATION AND KNOWLEDGE OF SALVATION

Illumination in the act of the Holy Spirit by which through the Word of God He inwardly prepares the mind of a sinner to receive the redemption of Christ. Its effect upon the individual is to give him the knowledge of his salvation.

The word illumination has been understood too exclusively in the sense of knowledge in theology. Sometimes the tendency has been to identify it with learning the doctrines taught in the Church. The New Testament words "enlighten" and "enlightenment" are broader than knowledge in their meaning. In biblical terminology "light" denotes that which belongs to the sphere of God. Cf. 1 Jn 1:5; 1 Tim 6:16. When God manifests Himself, that is light. Hence the revelation of God in Christ is called light, Lu 2:32; Jn 1:4; 3:19; 8:12. By contrast men are in darkness when they are alienated from God. From this darkness they are called through the gospel into the sphere of things divine, that is, light, Act 26:18; 1 Pet 2:9. So the gospel, which brings this revelation of God, is itself illumination, 2 Co 4:4. They who accept it become sons of light, Jn 12:36; 1 Th 5:5; Eph 5:8. The attainment of the knowledge of salvation is also illumination, Eph 1:18; 3:9; Heb 6:4. But this must not be understood merely as intellectual grasp of truth, but as a transference of the person into the sphere of the things of God. The Holy Spirit enlightens the soul by bringing God's love to bear upon it with all His grace.

According to this biblical usage illumination is not essentially different from vocation. The form of the conception is different. In vocation there is the idea of presenting to a sinner the glory and power of God's salvation; in illumination the idea is the manifestation of God upon the soul in sin and the dispelling of the evil there present. But in both there is the efficacious working of God in order to bring men into a saving relation to the Redeemer.

The illumination of a sinner by the Holy Spirit results in knowledge. It is not knowledge about God and Christ, but knowledge of God in Christ, 2 Co 4:6. It is knowledge of God as his God, with the love that forgives his sin, the mercy that cares for his miseries, and the grace that will lift him up out of sin into holiness. It is knowledge of God that is better described as being known by Him, Gal 4:9. He who has it, has the day-star in his heart, 2 Pet 1:19. This knowledge is also an opening of the eyes to the darkness of sin and the power of Satan, Act 26:18. It is, as is frequently said, knowledge of the law and the gospel, but knowledge of these as they apply to one's own condition.

REGENERATION AND CONSCIOUSNESS OF SALVATION

Regeneration is the act of the Holy Spirit by which He begins a new spiritual life in a person living the natural life of sin. The means are the Word of God and baptism. Since the new life towards God is the life of faith, regeneration is essentially the same as justification, only conceived as a new life under grace instead of a new juridical relation. The effect of regeneration is the consciousness of being a son of God and an heir of salvation.

The word regeneration is used in theology in different senses. It was so already in the sixteenth century. The Formula of Concord distinguishes three uses: (1) Equivalent to justification and renewal; (2) justification alone; (3) to renewal alone. The second use is here preferred, because it is closest to the New Testament use and also the use of the Reformers. It is the use of John Gerhard. It is important here to avoid all magical conceptions, approximating the conception of infused grace. Such a tendency showed itself in the notion, much favored by Lutheran theologians in the nineteenth century, that regeneration was an operation on the "nature" of man as contrasted with his mind, and may even be traced in the seventeenth century idea of conferring powers to believe (*vires credendi*).

The beginning of new spiritual life is represented by a number of expressions in the New Testament: regeneration, new birth, new creation, resurrection, quickening. It should be remembered that such expressions are figures of speech and that they are not to be taken in any physical sense. The idea running through them all is that when a sinner has received by faith God's sentence of life instead of the sentence of condemnation, he is a new man. This sentence of life is God's pardon for Christ's sake. This justification, the forgiveness of sins, is the passing from death unto life, Jn 5:24; 1 Jn 3:14. In Jn 3:3 Jesus tells of the new birth of water and the Spirit, and in verse 15 shows that it is actualized in faith in Himself. St. Paul uses the conception of regeneration, Tit 3:5, of new creation, 2 Co 5:17, Gal 6:15; of resurrection, Ro 6:4, Phil 3:10, Col 2:12; 3:1; and of quickening, Eph 2:5. In all of these instances the new state or life is a new relation to God by faith in the atoning death of Christ, out of which relation springs the renewal which is the new obedience. St. John speaks of a birth from God, which is bestowed upon believers as a right or privilege, Jn 1:12, 13; 1 Jn 2:29; 3:9; 4:7; 5:1, 4, 18. This birth is faith, but St. John is wont to combine justification and sanctification in his conception of "life," and therefore adds the fruits of faith. St. James and St. Peter speak of a begetting by the Word, Ja 1:18, 1 Pet 1:23, and the latter of a begetting by the resurrection of Christ, 1 Pet 1:3. In these instances faith is meant.

In the New Testament regeneration expresses a new relation, not an inward transformation. It is the gift of God's grace and forgiveness, therefore essentially the same as justification. But in faith the individual knows himself to be in this relation, and out of this faith spring the motives of holy living. Regeneration is personal, not physical nor magical.

Regeneration is experienced as the consciousness of salvation. This consciousness expresses itself in prayer and doing God's will. In the new relation of adoption, which the Holy Spirit certifies to the believer in Christ, the soul turns to the Father in all its needs, Ro 8:15; Gal 4:6. And conscious of being a child of God, the soul is impelled to be like the Father, as St. Paul says, to be an "imitator of God," Eph 5:1, doing such deeds as are seen in Christ.

CONVERSION AND REPENTANCE WITH SURRENDER TO GOD

Conversion is turning to God in repentance and faith. Viewed from the divine side, it is the act of the Holy Spirit by which He brings a sinner to faith in Christ. Viewed from the human side, it is the act of the sinner, under the operation of the grace of the Holy Spirit, turning to Christ in faith. It manifests itself in repentance and self-surrender to God.

Two New Testament words express conversion: "*epistrephein*" and "*metanoiein.*" The former is generally used of turning from idols or what is evil to God. The prominent thought is the religious idea of coming to God. "*Metanoia,*" translated repentance, is change of mind. It is used of the change from evil thinking and doing. The prominent thought is the moral idea of sorrow for sin. Both terms together constitute the biblical idea of conversion. Sometimes both are used in connection, Act 3:19; 26:20. Both are combined with believing, Act 11:21; 20:21; 26:18; Mk 1:15. Conversion includes both sorrow for and aversion to sin and coming to God, repentance and faith.

The Bible generally speaks of turning, not of being converted. The verb is intransitive. But the transitive idea is supported, not only by the general biblical truth that all that pertains to salvation comes from God, but by explicit scriptural statement in the use of the passive idea in several Old Testament passages, Jer 4:1; 31:18; Lam 5:21; Ez 34:16, and in the promise of a new heart which God will give, Jer 24:7; Ez 11:19; 36:26.

In ecclesiastical usage conversion sometimes comprehends both the spiritual change and its results in life and conduct; sometimes it is limited to the transition from a state of corruption to a state of grace. In the latter strict sense conversion is momentary, but in the broader sense it is not. The precise moment of conversion is probably never known. Some special experience connected with it may be remembered, but even this is not always the case. However, a converted man knows himself as such. As the true beginning of Christian life is in baptism, conversion as included in the grace of baptism may come before conscious experience in the case of infant baptism. But if the baptismal grace is not lost, the consciousness of conversion will come later, and often it comes with a painful awakening. Where there is a lapse from faith, the renewal of faith after repentance is possible. Conversion may be repeated.

Conversion manifests itself in repentance, which has been tersely described as recognizing, confessing, hating and forsaking sin. It manifests itself also in a surrender of one's self to God, the recognition that we are not our own, 1 Co 6:19, that we do not live to ourselves, Ro 14:7; 2 Co 5:15, that our lives are to be a living sacrifice to God, Ro 12:1, and that for His sake we are to deny ourselves, Mt 16:24.

SEALING AND CERTAINTY OF SALVATION

Sealing is the act of the Holy Spirit in which by His indwelling in the believer He assures him of his adoption, and is Himself the pledge of his heavenly inheritance. The inward experience of it is certainty of salvation.

It is not customary in dogmatics to make a special in the order of salvation of sealing, although the idea expressed by it is not passed over. On the other hand in the traditional treatment of the order of salvation a special place is assigned to what is called the Mystic Union. By this is meant the indwelling of God in the believer, as promised by the Savior in Jn 14:23. God works not only upon man from without, but is immanent in him in immediate fellowship of love. We join this truth of the mystic union with what the New Testament says of the sealing of the believer. For Christ and the Father are present in him through the Holy Spirit.

The figure of sealing is used in a number of applications in the Bible. It is St. Paul who applies it to the assurance of acceptance with God in justification, 2 Co 1:21, 22; Eph 1:13-14; 4:30. Prophets of old and Christ promised the Spirit. In faith the promised Spirit is received. The gospel is demonstration of the Spirit and of power, 1 Co 2:4. Those who receive the gospel in faith are epistles written with the Spirit of the living God, 2 Co 3:3. The Spirit dwelling in the heart is the seal of the truth of all God's saving promises to the believer. He is the earnest, the pledge and foretaste of the promised inheritance. Because the Word is the testimony of the Spirit, it works assurance. His indwelling is the realization of the mystic union with God, in which our fellowship is with the Father and with His Son Jesus Christ, 1 Jn 1:3.

The inward experience of God's sealing by the Spirit is the certainty of our salvation. The sure ground of our justification is never in our feelings, nor in the fruits of holiness which we may think we see in our lives. It is only in God's Word of promise. But that promise lives in our souls when the Holy Spirit lives in us. This is the testimony of the Holy Spirit which our fathers spoke of as the ultimate proof of the divine character of the Scriptures.

SANCTIFICATION AND STRIVING FOR HOLINESS

Sanctification is the act of the Holy Spirit by which the believer is consecrated to God and delivered from the dominion of sin. Its experience manifests itself in the endeavor to perfect holiness in the fear of the Lord.

In Luther's Catechism sanctification is the whole work of the application of grace by the Holy Spirit. In ordinary theological use it is the process and progress by which the believer approximates spiritual and moral perfection. Luther's use is nearer to that of the word in the Bible.

In the New Testament the word sanctification means a state of consecration to God. The idea is carried over from the Old Testament. Holiness is not man's achievement; it is God's gift, God's fitting a person to appear before Him. Into this state a sinner is brought when the redemption of Christ is applied to him, that is, when he is justified. In the New Testament use of the term sanctification does not mean a progress in holiness, much less a progress into holiness. So far as it includes the life of holiness which results from justification, it is the reaffirmation of the original consecration of the believer in Christ. It is the constant renewal of justification, just as justification is implicit sanctification. Believers have been sanctified once for all by the redemption of Christ, Heb 10:10, 14, 29. Sanctification is the appropriation of the righteousness of Christ to man for his salvation by the Holy Spirit, 1 P 1:2; 1 Th 4:7; 2 Th 2:13; Ro 6:19, 20. The same act of grace that brought justification brought sanctification, 1 Co 1:30. Hence believers are holy in Christ, for in Him their sins are washed away. They are called saints and sanctified, Act 20:32; 26:18; 1 Co 1:2; Heb 2:11; 10:10.

But while sanctification, as the word is used in the New Testament, is not a progress but a state, it is everywhere implied that it shall unfold in deeds of holiness. There is no scriptural foundation for the theory of a complete instantaneous perfection and ceasing from sin. Sanctification is not a "second blessing" which follows the first grace of justification. It is a consecration to God by faith and a state of cleansing from sin by Christ's atonement. Nowhere is it intimated in the New Testament that any man has personally risen to the level of righteousness imputed to Him by God for Christ's sake. St. Paul at the close of his life distinctly disclaimed it.

Renovation is a New Testament synonym of sanctification, Tit 3:5; Col 3:10. When we are renewed in Christ, by His forgiveness of our sin, we thereby pass from a state of sin to a state of righteousness. The renewal is first forgiveness, then the fruits of it. The new man, of whom St. Paul speaks, does not become such by his good deeds, but by the grace of Christ; but being a new man in Christ he brings forth the fruits of goodness.

The working out of this sanctification and renewal, which is put upon the sinner by grace when he believes in Christ, into an unfolded life of righteousness and holiness, is what is meant by sanctification, as the word is commonly used. The idea is altogether scriptural. Progress in holy living is taught in all that is said in the Scriptures of the conflict of the Spirit with the flesh, Gal 5 :17; of the fruits of the Spirit, Gal 5:22; of crucifying the flesh, Gal 5:24; Col 3:5; of taking the cross, Mt 16:24; of putting on the new man, Eph 4:24; of thinking on things virtuous, Phil 4:8; and of growing in grace, 1 Pet 2:2. The believer is consecrated to God by the sacrifice of Christ; therefore he must live unto God.

PRESERVATION AND PERSEVERANCE

Preservation is the act of the Holy Spirit by which He supplies all needed grace to the believer to stand steadfast in the faith and to resist all temptations to fall from it. By it the believer is enabled and incited to persevere in the life of faith in Christ.

Salvation is by grace in its continuance as well as in its beginning. Faith always leans upon God. It cannot stand otherwise. The best expression of the grace of preservation is found in the words of St. Paul: "He who began a good work in you will perfect it until the day of Jesus Christ," Phil 1:6. The same apostle eloquently expressed the triumphant assurance of the preserving love of God, which never forsakes the redeemed in Christ, Ro 8:35-39. It is God's faithfulness, which will never let us be tempted above our ability, that comes into consideration here, 1 Co 10:13. This faithfulness is not fate. It does not preclude the possibility of falling from grace, Ro 11:22. As we are justified by faith, so we also stand by faith, Ro 11:20. The conditions which make God's preserving grace our only security and defense are our weakness and the temptations that are in the world. "Lead us not into temptation." This is the prayer for preserving grace.

The grace of preservation received into the heart is the gift of perseverance. It is the constancy of regenerated will. From the position of absolute predestination perseverance becomes necessity. The elect must without fail in the end rise out of all trials and lapses into true faith. The erroneous assumption in this is that some men (the elect) cannot frustrate the work of grace in them. But perseverance is not necessity; it is voluntary abiding in the love of God by the grace which God supplies. It is manifested in patience in trials, endurance in warfare with sin, and in watchfulness against temptation. It strengthens itself by continuing in the Word of God and in prayer.

PERFECTING AND THE CHRISTIAN IDEAL

Perfecting is the act of the Holy Spirit by which He shapes the believer into complete manhood of faith. In it the Christian becomes conscious of the ideal of life in Christ.

We are not speaking of the state of moral perfection, but of Christian maturity. There are babes in Christ, 1 Co 3:1, and there are full-grown men in Christ, Col 1:28. Both are in the faith, but only the mature believer knows what it really means to be a Christian. Christian maturity is a work of the Holy Spirit. In the Christian life we do not attain maturity by mere years, but by the assimilation of the grace of the Holy Spirit, ministered to us in the Word of God. The mature Christian is not sinless, but with his faults and weaknesses he has such fullness of development and strength of spiritual understanding and will that, as St. Paul expresses it, he stands perfect and fully assured in all the will of God, Col 4:12.

The study of the use of the Greek word "*teleios*" in the New Testament will show what is meant by the perfecting here spoken of. That word is sometimes translated perfect, but its real meaning is complete, and it has special reference to completeness of growth. The moral idea in it is not so much the negative quality of the absence of sin as the positive quality of the possession of the attributes and qualifications for goodness. The word is contrasted with babes or children. Cf. 1 Co 14 :20, Heb 5:14. Christian maturity manifests itself in knowledge, Eph 4:13, in capacity to receive wisdom, 1 Co 2:6, and in firmness of mind and character generally, Phil 3:12. So the word is used in our Lord's familiar saying, Mt 5:48, and in Mt 19:21.

The mature Christian knows his ideal. He may have much yet to learn to perfect his ideal. St. Paul near the close of his life felt that he had not yet attained his full growth, Phil 3:12; but his ideal was before him and to that he pressed on. In regard to his Christian ideal he had no misgivings. He knew what he aspired to be, or rather what he was laid hold on by Jesus Christ for.

The ideal of Christian life has rarely been correctly conceived in the Church. There is usually some one-sidedness noticeable in the trend of life in the Church in every period. The two opposite errors which need most to be avoided are flight from the world and overvaluation of present world interests. The early and medieval Church inclined to the former error, the modern Church inclines to the latter error. The Reformation, in opposition to false monastic ideals, stressed the value of life's vocations in family, state and human society. Cf. for example what is said on perfection in the Augsburg Confession, Article 27, 49. The Christian ideal of perfection, as we see it, consists not in merely passing through things temporal, but in working in all good things temporal so as not to lose things eternal.

CHAPTER IX
THE CHURCH AND THE MEANS OF GRACE

THE APPLICATION OF REDEMPTION BY THE HOLY SPIRIT IN THE CHURCH THROUGH THE MEANS OF GRACE

THE CHURCH

The grace of the Holy Spirit is applied for salvation in the Church, which consists of those who by faith have entered into fellowship with God through Christ. Through their communion with God they have fellowship with one another. Therefore the Church is defined as the communion or congregation of believers. This assembly of believers is continuously being brought into existence by the preaching of the Word of God and the administration of the sacraments. These are therefore the essential marks by which the presence of the Church is known.

The conception of the Church in the New Testament is rooted in the Old Testament idea of the covenant people. Israel was a nation and Israel was a priesthood, realizing its priestly character through an institutional priesthood and ceremonial. But the national and institutional organization was not essential to its existence as the people of God, for during the captivity it continued without these. Israel was essentially a community of faith in Jehovah. Therefore the distinction, so succinctly stated by St. Paul, that not all are Israel who are of Israel, Ro 9:6, was anticipated in the prophets. In the New Testament the Church is the people of God, 1 Pet 2:10, the Israel of God, Gal 6:16, made up of believers from Jews and Gentiles, Eph 2:12,19.

Therefore what was said of Israel in its relation to God at the founding of the covenant, Ex 19:6, is directly applied to the Church. It is the elect race, the royal priesthood, the holy nation, the people for God's own possession, 1 Pet 2:9. Israel in assembly was "*kahal*," the congregation. In contrast with the "*kahal*" of the Jewish people, our Savior declared that He would build His Church upon the foundation of faith in Himself, Mt 16:18. The Greek name for church is ecclesia, originally meaning an assembly of citizens, Act 19:32. Jesus spoke of His Church only twice, so far as the record shows. He generally spoke of the kingdom of God. The question has been raised whether Jesus ever intended to found an organization. We have no express teaching from Him in this direction. But certain facts in His work show that He contemplated a separate organization of His Church. He gathered His disciples into a separate flock, Lu 12:32, Jn 10:16; He committed to them the observance of outward ordinances, baptism and His Supper; and He foresaw and foretold the opposition of the Jews, which would make a separation of His disciples from them necessary; and He promised His presence among them in a way to imply a close association among themselves. But He Himself instituted no constitution or form of government for them. That was left to the wisdom of His disciples.

In its separate existence the Church was founded on the day of Pentecost. After that day the name Church was regularly applied to the body of the disciples of Christ, as the book of Acts and the Epistles show. The Church is the body of Christ, Eph 1:23; 4:12, the body which He created, and of which He is the life and the head. The term church in the New Testament sometimes refers to the body of disciples generally, sometimes to those in one locality, always conceived as in this world. The New Testament does not speak of the Church triumphant, although it points to the triumph of God's people.

The bond of union in the Church is not outward. What Christ promised to His disciples as the bond of their union was the Holy Spirit, Act 1:5; Jn 20 :22. So St. Paul declares the unity of the Church to be the unity of the Spirit, Eph 4:3. All in the Church have access to the Father in one Spirit, Eph 2:18. All who entered the Church by baptism were baptized into one body in one Spirit, 1 Co 12:13. But the Spirit comes to men through the Word of God, which is also applied in baptism and in the communion of the Lord's Supper. Therefore the unity of the Spirit is a union in the believing use of the Word and sacraments of God.

The object of the Church is not merely to be an institution of salvation. It exists to express the common fellowship of believers with God through Christ. Worship is the manifestation of its life. Worship of believers in common is the necessary expression of their common relation to God. But in its life of communion with God the Church necessarily exhibits the salvation which Christ has brought into the world. It is itself the representation of it, Eph 5:25. To make known this salvation to others is a mission laid upon it by its Lord. It is to hold forth the Word of life. The Church then is both an institution of worship and an institution of salvation.

The word institution at once suggests something that has outward shape. But the Church is a union in faith. Its bond of union is inward. But the inward life in the Spirit manifests itself in external forms. The Lord Himself put the outward side to the Church in the institution of Word and sacrament, as the means through which the life of the Church is nourished, sustained and molded. The Church is (to imitate a German compound) spirit-bodily. The essential feature of the outward manifestation of the Church is not organization (that may be of diverse form), but ministration of Word and sacrament. As an institution the Church is the institution of the means of grace.

From the conception of the Church as a spiritual body realizing itself in outward form the distinction of visible and invisible as applied to the Church becomes clear. The visible and the invisible Church is not two churches, but one body. The Church is invisible in that the bond of faith is inward and spiritual; but it is visible in that the essential marks of the Church, Word and sacrament, and their use can be sensibly located. Under the false conception of absolute predestination the distinction of the invisible and visible Church becomes the distinction between the elect and the body of professing Christians. That really makes two bodies. The distinction between visible and invisible Church has no real significance in the Roman Catholic conception, for in it the Church is identified with the organization of which the Pope is the head, and which, as Bellarmine said, is as palpable as the kingdom of France.

To see how the definition of the Church squares with the actual aggregate of Christendom in the world and the empirical institutional forms of the Church involves difficulty. The actual situation is that many are associated with true believers in the profession of faith and the use of the means of grace, who are not believers. Do they belong to the Church? If not, what is their relation to it? The light of grace shines not only upon the body of true believers, but creates a penumbra around it. What is the relation of this obscurity to the Church? Scholastic Lutheran theology, which had to deal with a State church, drew a distinction between two assemblies: that of believers (*coetus credentium*) and that of the called, i.e., the invited (*coetus vocatorum*). In this distinction the believers are not outside of the called. There are two circles, a larger circle of the called and within it a smaller circle of believers. The latter alone is really the Church. Still in some sense all in the larger circle are attached to the Church. The danger in such a distinction is that it may suggest a double Church, which is not at all its intention. The environment around the body of true believers is not Church, it is the nearer sphere in which the Church is realizing itself more fully.

Five attributes of the Church are of doctrinal importance: one, holy, catholic, apostolic, and alone saving. Early in the history of the Church it became customary to refer these to the external organization of the Church, as is still done in the Roman Catholic body. Protestants, with a spiritual conception of the Church, necessarily judge of these attributes from the inward essence, not from the outward form of the Church. As to unity, the Church is one in its faith and in the possession of the essential means of the life of the Church, Word and sacraments. As to holiness, it is holy, not in the sinless purity of its members, but in the sanctification which it receives by grace from its Head through the Holy Spirit. The Church is catholic because it embraces all believers everywhere. Incidentally it should be remarked that believers in Christ may be found in church organizations whose official teaching is erroneous or which have become corrupted. The Church is apostolic, not by any apostolic succession of bishops (for which there is no foundation in Scripture or in history), but by the continuance in it of the apostolic teaching as found in the Scriptures. Finally, the principle that outside of the Church there is no salvation is

true, because there is no salvation but in Christ, whom the
Church confesses and teaches. It is not true of any church
organization. Alone saving is the attribute of the Church as
the communion of believers. The Augsburg Confession notes
as a characteristic of the Church, that it shall continue
forever. This is based on the promise of Christ and upon the
unfailing efficacy of the Gospel to make believers in all ages.

THE MINISTRY

The Church, in its communion with God and in its winning of souls, is
bound to the preaching of the Word of God and the administration of the
sacraments. Therefore a ministry of the Gospel is necessary. Moreover,
the Church manifests its faith in manifold activities for its own
upbuilding and for the welfare of mankind. All this makes it necessary
for the Church to organize itself in some form of polity. But all orders
and ranks of the ministry and all regulations for organization are
human ordinances.

No form of ministry or church polity is prescribed in the
New Testament. The apostolic office is an apparent
exception to this statement. But it is not prescribed that the
apostolic office should continue in the Church. It could not
be perpetuated. The name apostle was used in the early
Church for any preacher who carried the Gospel from place
to place in the name of the Lord. Instances of this loose use
of the name are found in the New Testament also. Cf. 2 Co
11:5, 13; 12:11; Rev 2:2 ; Act 14:14; 1 Th 2:6. But in the strict
sense of the name, the office was singular. The apostles were
appointed before the founding of the Church and for its
founding. The permanent element in the apostleship was not
the office itself, but the preaching of the Gospel. No form of

ministry is prescribed in the New Testament, although a diversity of forms is exemplified in it. A comparison of earlier and later epistles, for instance Corinthians with the pastoral epistles, shows a development in the forms of the ministry in apostolic times. The earlier epistles distinguish gifts rather than offices. Cf. for example, Ro 12:6; Eph 4:11.

The priestly character of all believers is fundamental in regard to ministerial duties, 1 Pet 2:5, 9; Rev 1:6; Ro 12:1; Heb 13:15. All believers have the same Spirit, but the gifts of the Spirit are diverse and individual, 1 Co 12:4. Hence there were diversities of ministration, i.e., different activites in the Church, but at first not different official positions. The gift determined the work. But offices soon became necessary. A beginning is made at Jerusalem with deacons for the care of the poor, Act 6:5. Soon we read of elders at Jerusalem, possibly on the synagogue model, Act 11:30. Then we read of elders also in missionary churches, Act 14:23. These are identical with bishops, Act 20:17, 28. In the pastoral epistles the offices of bishops or elders and deacons are fully developed. The ministry of the Word did not belong exclusively to the elders, perhaps it was not their principal function at all. But there were elders who taught the Word, 1 Tim 3:2; Tit 1:9.

From these New Testament facts we learn that to understand the nature of the ministry we must not begin with the office as a position or rank in the Church. We must start with the broad basis of the means of grace. God gave Word and sacrament. He also gave gifts. But He appointed no order of men for the ministry. The appointment of those who were to minister was left to the wisdom of the Church. The ministry of the Church is the office of the means of grace. This ministry is of divine institution, but it was committed by the Lord to no class in the Church, but to the Church itself. The Church itself, according to the wisdom given to it, designates those who shall exercise this ministry for it. The preaching of the Gospel is the preaching of the Church, not a private power or prerogative of a minister. Baptism and communion are sacraments of the Church, not individual operations of a privileged person. In the work of administering the Word of God according to arising needs and circumstances the Church appoints ministers for different functions, one a pastor, another a missionary, another a teacher, and it may be appoints to them different degrees of jurisdiction and authority, for instance a president of a synod or a superintendent, whom it may call bishop. But that which is common and essential in all such offices and ranks is the one office of the means of grace. This is the divinely appointed element; the other features are variable. In this sense there is parity of ministers of the Gospel.

In the Roman Catholic conception of the ministry, and in fact wherever the doctrine of apostolic succession is held, there is a divinely privileged rank or order of men, to whom alone the administration of grace is committed, and from whom the body of the Church must receive it. This is really the creation of a higher Church within the Church, a Church possessed of the endowments of grace in contrast with the Church of professing believers. This false development began early in the history of the Church. The fundamental error gained recognition at the end of the second century, when the gifts of the Holy Spirit, notably the *charisma veritatis*, the charism of the truth, was conceived as being lodged in the bishops instead of the body of believers.

The presbyterial system, developed by Calvin, is judicial rather than ministrative of grace. It is a divinely ordered system for the government and discipline of the Church. It is based upon the erroneous assumption that what is found existing in the Church in the New Testament is a divine prescription for the Church in all times.

But besides the direct dispensation of Word and sacrament the Church engages in manifold activities for its own upbuilding and for the welfare of its members and of mankind. The ultimate aim of all this activity is the spiritual good of men. For these activities it makes such provision of official appointment as the needs of the work and its own wisdom dictate. So, for example, the ministry of mercy has gained recognition along with the ministry of the Word.

Ordination by prayer and laying on of hands is a solemn confirmation of the call to the ministry by the Church, for which there are New Testament examples. The act as such confers no official character, except in so far as it is regarded as the completion of the call. But the prayers in it and the imposition of hands are expressions of faith in God, which obtain His blessing.

THE MEANS OF GRACE

The grace of the Holy Spirit is applied to men through divinely appointed instrumentalities, viz., the Word of God and the sacraments of baptism and the Lord's Supper. These are therefore called the means of grace.

Means of grace are not everything that may be helpful in religious life. They are means through which grace is conferred. As grace comes by the will and gift of God alone, the means of grace must be of His appointment. Word and sacrament are the only means of this character. In theology faith has been called the subjective means of grace. It does not confer, but appropriates grace. Prayer is not a means of grace. It may be called a means to grace, since it seeks grace and has God's promise.

The power of the means of grace is grounded in the presence of Christ in the Church and His giving the Spirit. The revelation of salvation in Christ was not a transaction historically completed with the life of Christ on earth, of which the Scriptures contain only a historical record. It is the manifestation of a present salvation, to which the living Christ ever gives efficacy through the Holy Spirit. The activity of the Holy Spirit, revealing Christ and His riches to men, is not a secret inward working in the hearts of men, but an openly manifested operation upon them as personalities. It is made manifest in the Word, which declares salvation, and in the sacraments, which Christ appointed for the application of salvation. The idea of inward operations of the Spirit without external means of grace, held by mystics and enthusiasts, has no place in Lutheran theology. And with good reason. The application of grace for salvation is a different thing from prophetic and apostolic illumination and inspiration. Faith cometh by hearing and hearing by the Word of God. This is the apostolic principle that governs in this case. The New Testament knows of no mediation of salvation or grace-bringing work of the Spirit except through the Gospel.

The operation of the means of grace is not magical. It is personal. It is mediated by faith. Roman Catholic theology ascribes to the sacraments the power to impart grace *ex opere operato*. This is a magical idea. It is connected with the conception of grace as a thing that can be infused like a physical substance. Approaching the Roman Catholic conception of infused grace is an idea taught by many prominent Lutheran theologians in the last century, according to which the sacraments, in distinction from the Word which acts upon the mind, act directly upon the "nature." So baptism is supposed to introduce into the "nature" a germ of life and redemptive potencies, and the Lord's Supper is supposed to prepare the resurrection body. This idea must be rejected. The action of the means of grace is not physical or hyperphysical, but spiritual, calling for personal response.

THE WORD OF GOD

All saving relations of God to a sinner are mediated by the Word of God, through which He declares His gracious will and salvation. This Word is in itself efficacious to produce faith, because it conveys not only knowledge, but also grace that convicts, converts and confirms. It is the means through which the Holy Spirit works upon the heart.

"Faith cometh by hearing and hearing by the Word of God," Ro 10:17. This is the teaching of Scripture from beginning to end. To the patriarchs God spoke; to Moses and the prophets of the Old Testament the Word of the Lord was given; in the New Testament Christ proclaimed His gospel and sent His disciples to preach it. There is no instance of faith being given without the Word.

The phrase Word of God is the standing designation for the revelation of God in the New Testament. It is used regularly in the epistles and the book of Acts; it is also used in the gospels and by Christ Himself; it is used in the Old Testament. The name is significant of the power in the Word.

The Word is the chief means of grace, in a sense the only means of grace; for the sacraments are only modifications of the Word. Hence they are called the visible Word. By the Word is meant not the mere phraseology of the

Scriptures (there is nothing magical about Bible phraseology, although it has reverent associations), but the truth contained in the Bible put to use in anybody's language, whether by translation, reading, exposition or free utterance. Therefore preaching and teaching that agree with the Word of God in the Bible are also the Word of God. The Bible is not the Word of God in a material or mechanical manner. Not used, it is not a word.

The efficacy of the Word of God, on which its power as a means of grace depends, presupposes its inspiration. For its power is not the power of human eloquence or persuasion, but lies in the supernatural working of the Holy Spirit, who first inspired the Word and is still in it.

> My speech and my preaching were not in persuasive words of wisdom, but in demonstration of the Spirit and of power: that your faith should not stand in the wisdom of men, but in the power of God (1 Co 2:4-5).

The Word as such is the testimony of the Holy Spirit, whose power is in it. When a person hears the Word of God, the Holy Spirit does not come to him with a special inward revelation to make it efficacious and saving truth for him, as if apart from such a special operation of the Spirit the Word were only a tinkling cymbal and sounding brass. The power of the Word evidences itself in the heart as the testimony of the Holy Spirit, Ro 8:16; Gal 4:6. For he that has hid the Word in his heart has the testimony of the Spirit in himself. This truth that the Spirit speaks to man through the Word is distinctive of Lutheran doctrine; for outside of the Lutheran Church the action of the Spirit is conceived as only concurrent with the use of the Word, and sometimes not concurrent.

As a means of grace the Word produces repentance and faith. In the former respect, as giving knowledge of sin, it is law; in the latter respect, as offering pardon and peace, it is gospel. The distinction of law and gospel is the distinction of divine demand and divine promise. In the Old Testament law predominates, in the New Testament gospel.

Discussions in the period of the Reformation on the relation of the regenerate man to the law led to a distinction of several uses of the law. Usually three uses are distinguished: pedagogical, civil, and didactic. The term pedagogical has reference to St. Paul's declaration that the law is a schoolmaster or tutor to Christ. The term elenchtic, meaning convicting, has reference to St. Paul's declaration that by the law is the knowledge of sin. The first use of the law then is its use to effect repentance. The civil use is the use to regulate moral conduct in domestic and social life. The didactic use is the use to instruct regenerate persons in the principles of holy living. This last use is designed to explain the somewhat intricate question of the believer's relation to the law. It is explicit New Testament teaching that the believer is not under the law. In what sense is he free from it? Is he above the law? To put the believer under the law is legalism; to put him above it is antinomianism. Both are errors. No man is above the law. The believer constantly needs to learn what the will of God is in life's conduct, and this he learns from the law. Hence the didactic use. But the impulses to right life in the believer are not legal, but spiritual. The New Testament, especially St. Paul in Ro 8:1 and Gal 5:16, teaches that the believer is impelled by the Spirit to fulfill the righteousness of the law. So the doctrine of faith establishes the law, Ro 3:31. The principle of life in the believer is no longer the law, but the Spirit; but the form of the life is defined in the law.

There is one use of the gospel which requires special remark, the Word of absolution. Absolution, as practiced in the Church, is an application of the Word of God for the forgiveness of sins, in one respect like the sacraments: it also is an individualizing of God's grace. For this reason it is grouped with the sacraments of baptism and the Lord's Supper in the Augsburg Confession and the Apology.

HOLY BAPTISM

Baptism is the ordinance of Christ by which a sinner is initiatively received into participation in His redemption. By it are conferred the Holy Spirit, the forgiveness of sins, regeneration and entrance into the Church of Christ. The personal appropriation of these blessings is conditioned on faith. Age is never a disqualification for baptism.

From the verb "*baptizein*," which signifies to immerse or to wash in some other way (Lu 11:38; Mk 7:4), two nouns are derived, both of which are used in the New Testament : "*baptismos*," signifying washing generally, and "*baptisma*," which became the specific religious act of baptism. Adumbrations of Christian baptism are found in the Old Testament in circumcision and in the washings prescribed in the law. Perhaps the Jewish baptism of proselytes was also an anticipation. A more direct preparation was the baptism of John, which differed from Old Testament ablutions both in form and purpose. The washings of the law were self-washings; John's baptism was applied by another. The washings of the law were purifications to fit the person to appear before God; John's baptism was a symbol of repentance, looking to the forgiveness that was to be revealed in the approaching Kingdom of God. It did not, like Christian baptism, confer the Holy Spirit, Mt 3:11.

Christian baptism was instituted by Christ after His resurrection, Mt 28:19, and was first exercised on the day of Pentecost, Act 2:38. The baptizing previously performed by the disciples of Christ was the baptism of John, Jn 4:2. In the conversation with Nicodemus Jesus, with obvious reference to John's baptism, speaks of the need and significance of such an ordinance as He afterwards instituted, a baptism of new birth through the Holy Spirit upon the basis of His atonement. The teaching of the New Testament shows that baptism is a means of participating in the blessings of Christ's redemption.

This is the significance of baptizing in the name of the Father and the Son and the Holy Spirit. Whatever of grace that Triune Name stands for becomes the possession of the person baptized. Baptism confers the Holy Spirit and remission of sins, and thereby regeneration and entrance into the Church. St. Peter names the first two in his address on the day of Pentecost, Act 2:38. The general idea of remission of sins in baptism is variously expressed: as a sprinkling from an evil conscience, Heb 10:22; a sprinkling with the blood of Christ, 1 Pet 1:2; an obtaining of a good conscience, 1 Pet 3:21; a washing away of sin, Act 22:16; a saving by the washing of regeneration, Tit 3:5; a washing for justification and sanctification, 1 Co 6:11. The gift of the Holy Spirit in baptism is also variously stated: it is a baptism in the Spirit, 1 Co 12:13; a renewing effected by the Holy Spirit, Tit 3:5. As the Holy Spirit is the bond of union with Christ, baptism is an insertion into Christ, an entering into the fruits of His death and resurrection, Col 2:11, 12; Ro 6:3, 4; Gal 3:27. In the first age of the Church the charisms of the Holy Spirit were sometimes conferred with baptism, Act 19:5-6, but in the exceptional case of Cornelius the gifts of the Spirit preceded the baptism, Act 10:44. The gift of the Holy Spirit with the remission of sins constitutes regeneration. The entire blessing of salvation is conferred in baptism, Mk 16:16. Baptism has a relation to the Church. The Church is said to be cleansed by the washing of water with the Word, because it is made up of baptized believers, Eph 5:26. As the antitype of circumcision, Col 2:11, baptism is entrance into the new covenant with God and therefore an initiation into the Church, an initiation which even the miraculously converted Paul received.

On its internal side, then, baptism is the gift of Holy Spirit making personal the redemption of Christ. On its external side baptism is the application of water together with the Word of God that declares the saving grace of the Trinity. The quantity of water is unessential, as is also the mode of applying it, whether by immersion, pouring or sprinkling. But a conjunction of the Word with the water is essential, for by the sacramental union of the water with the Word baptism becomes a means of grace. Some of the scholastic Lutheran theologians tried to distinguish a terrestrial and a celestial material in baptism after the analogy of the Lord's Supper. The terrestrial material, water, was easy enough to define; but when it came to defining the celestial material there was guessing. Some thought it was the divine Word, others the Holy Spirit, still others the blood of Christ, and others again a special presence of the Trinity. Certainly all of these are related to baptism, but none of them is a celestial material like the body and blood of Christ in the Supper. It was therefore a wise thought of Baier in the seventeenth century to drop the whole idea of a celestial material in baptism.

Stated in a single word the effect of baptism is regeneration. But regeneration must not be conceived as a moral transformation of the person, least of all as a magical insertion of an embryonic spiritual life into the constitution of man. Regeneration is the creation of a relation of fellowship of God with man by the forgiveness of sins for Christ's sake. Therefore Luther's answer to the question in regard to the effect of baptism in the Small Catechism is of great significance. He says: "It works forgiveness of sins." When the Scriptures ascribe the effect of regeneration to baptism, it is in the same sense in which that effect is ascribed to the Word, namely, a new relation to God by faith, a relation of adoption by justification. If this relation of grace has already been effected through the Word, baptism confirms it.

Some persons have difficulty in understanding that regeneration is bestowed upon infants in baptism. On this subject we insert here a translation of a passage from the article on Regeneration in Meusel's *Kirchenlexikon*, which we heartily approve. After explaining that by regeneration an individual enters into a new relation to God, which is necessarily followed by a new course of conduct, the article continues:

> From this it appears how children can be regenerated in baptism. If one becomes a child of God without his own doing by grace through justification and adoption in Christ, then baptism is in principle the justification and reception of the individual into the state of grace of a Christian, God's act by which He

effects the adoption as His child upon the man, and there is no reason why God should not also receive children and them particularly into His grace and communion, and should not be able to endow them with the Spirit of adoption and actually do so. The fact that at first they have no consciousness of the new relation into which they enter by baptism cannot hinder the establishment of this relation, which proceeds altogether from God, nor their capacity for it, but it only obligates those who have their education in charge to awaken this consciousness, so that the new relation may become a personally appropriated possession and then may unfold its full blessing and benefit, whereas it remains a dead treasure without later conscious faith. How far the Holy Spirit, who according to the Scriptures is always communicated in and with the adoption as a child of God, the Spirit of adoption, also works upon the unconscious life of the infant, this remains a mystery as infant life generally is for us. There are different grades of communication of the Spirit according to the receptivity of individuals, and children receive it according to their measure, whereby it is self-evident that He can effect the full religious and ethical renewal only when the moral personality of the child has developed and unfolded itself. But this renewal grows organically out of the received baptismal grace and gift.

The saving effect of baptism is not due to the water, but to the efficacy of the Word which is combined with the water in its application. The efficacy is inherent in the sacrament as

God's ordinance, but the beneficial effect is dependent upon the faith of the person who receives the baptism. As the application of grace by baptism is not for the moment, but for the whole life, the faith may follow after a long interval of time and still appropriate the grace applied in baptism. Therefore one who receives baptism without faith and afterwards comes to faith is not baptized again. His baptism is effectual. Or if a person falls from faith after baptism and again returns to it, he is not baptized again; he simply returns to the relation with God vouchsafed to him in baptism.

The necessity for baptism lies in Christ's command. Its need arises from original sin and the actual sins which flow from it. Baptism removes the guilt of all sin, original and actual, but it does not extirpate concupiscence nor destroy its sinfulness. It washes away its guilt. Ideally it is the death of sin in every respect; for the whole salvation of Christ is appropriated in baptism. But the fruits of baptism are personally made the believer's own throughout his entire life of faith.

The necessity of baptism for infants is the same as for adults: in the command of Christ and their sinfulness. The right of infant baptism is founded upon Scriptural truths: first, the Savior never limited baptism for a specific class. He says: "all nations." Infants cannot be excluded. Secondly, Christ himself received children as proper subjects of the kingdom of God. The church follows his example. The chief difficulty of infant baptism is in understanding how they believe. Roman Catholic theology, following Augustine, imputes the faith of parents to the infant. Lutheran theology rejects this because one person cannot believe for another. Luther's notion, which has been followed by he Lutheran church, was to ascribe to the infant a faith of its own which is given by the Holy Spirit, through the prayer of the sponsors. It is difficult to conceive of this faith psychologically. It can only be a receptivity commensurate with the stage of that child's life. It is arbitrary to assume thatthe beginning of the religious life is conditioned by a certain degree of intellectual development. In its way the infant is as receptive of God's love as the adult. After all the solution of the matter is not to be sought in definitions of the possibility of infant faith, but in the power of God's gracious action. In baptism God adopts sinful adults as His children; why not infants? If faith in the full sense is inconceivable in infants, the promise of salvation may still be sealed to them with reference to future faith, in which the child is to be brought up.

THE LORD'S SUPPER

The redemption of Christ is also applied by means of the Lord's Supper, in which the body and blood of Christ are imparted in sacramental union with the elements of bread and wine, according to Christ's word. This sacrament is received in its entirety by all who receive the elements; but only those who receive it in faith appropriate the forgiveness of sins, of which the communicated body and blood are the pledge.

The nature and purpose of the Lord's Supper is explained in the institution of Christ itself. Other Scripture references, like those of St. Paul in 1 Co 10:16 and 11:26 or our Lord's discourse on the bread of life in the sixth chapter of St. John, cannot be made the foundation, with which the words of the institution must then be made to accord. Rather these can only be used for sidelights on what the institution declares itself to be. The four accounts of the institution in Mt 26:26, Mk 14:22; Lu 22:19 and 1 Co 11:23 show variations of text, which create critical questions. From the absence of a distinct injunction of Christ in Matthew and Mark to repeat the act, and from the dependence of St. Luke's record upon St. Paul, it has been argued that the Lord never intended to institute a rite that was to be observed in the Church. But the fact is that the sacrament was observed in the Church from the earliest years, as the epistle to the Corinthians proves, a circumstance unthinkable without a command of the Lord. Moreover, St. Paul states explicitly the command: "Do this in remembrance of me." His authority is sufficient.

Notwithstanding the textual variations in the four accounts of the institution all vital points are clear. By the language of the institution and its circumstances the Supper is connected with the death of Christ. The Lord deals with His Body given for His disciples and His blood shed for many for the remission of sins. In some way the sacrifice on the cross for the remission of sins is applied to His own in the Supper. How? There can be no question but that the bread and wine are symbols. But are they nothing more? The Lord says that what He gives to eat is His body and the wine in the cup is His blood of the New Testament. Is this to be received literally? There is no reason to doubt that the Lord is able to make His word good. And the circumstances indicate that He was not engaged in a symbolic communion. There is, first, the connection with the passover, which Christ brought to an end by this act. The Old Testament passover was eaten: so the New Testament passover, Christ, was given to be eaten for participation in the redemption effected by it. In the second place, Christ established a new covenant or testament in His blood. The Supper does not symbolize it as something about to be accomplished; but realizes it by imparting the body and blood on which it is founded. Finally, the solemnity of this testamental act under the shadow of the cross at the hour of Christ's leave taking from His disciples precludes the idea of mere unexplained symbolic representations.

The words of the institution must be taken to mean that Christ imparts His body and blood in the Supper. This impartation takes place in the eating of the bread and the drinking of the wine. What St. Paul says confirms this interpretation. He calls the sacrament the communion of the body and blood of the Lord, 1 Co 10:16. He designates the cup and the bread as this communion, that is, the eating and drinking make the communion. He declares that an unworthy use of the cup and the bread is guilt against the body and blood of the Lord, 1 Co 11:27. This implies their presence in the sacrament. The discourse of Christ on the bread of life in Jn 6:53 is not a discourse on the Supper, but on the general truth of faith-fellowship with Himself. In such faith-fellowship there is a mystic union with Christ, an eating of His flesh and a drinking of His blood. This faith-fellowship with Christ is specialized in the Supper as a communion with the real body and blood of the Lord by eating and drinking these, where the Lord appointed them to be received.

In the communion there is then a sacramental union of the bread and wine and the body and blood of Christ. This sacramental union rests upon the institution of Christ. It is not made by faith. The faith of the administrant or that of the recipient do not make it, nor does absence of faith in either unmake it. It depends upon Christ's word alone. Hence unworthy communicants and those who receive it without faith also receive the body and blood, but they receive it not for blessing, but for judgment, 1 Co 11:29, not discriminating the Lord's body from common bread. For the beneficial effect of receiving the body and blood of Christ depends upon faith.

The reception of the body and blood of Christ causes no magical effect upon the person. The body and blood are pledges of redemption, sealing the promise of the remission of sins. There is a danger of lapsing into physical notions inapplicable here. In ancient times and in some recent writers we find the idea that the reception of the body of Christ has the effect of preparing the resurrection body in the person of the believer. There is no scriptural support for such an idea. If it is held in a materializing form, it is to be rejected. In the sense that the believer is being prepared for resurrection by all the grace he receives in Christ and so also in the communion, it is without doubt true, but of no special importance in regard to the sacrament.

In the Lord's Supper there is an earthly material, bread and wine, and a celestial material, the body and blood of Christ. The doctrine of transubstantiation identifies these; that of consubstantiation or impanation confuses and mingles them; the symbolic doctrine separates them; the Lutheran doctrine of real presence unites them. The Lutheran Church holds to a sacramental union, unique in its nature, of the terrestrial and the celestial, but only in the sacramental act of eating and drinking. "No sacrament apart from use." This old rule precludes every idea approaching the Roman Catholic doctrine that the body and blood are permanently in the elements, so that they can be exhibited for adoration in the mass and in eucharistic processions. The doctrine of sacramental union is opposed to the Reformed doctrine, according to which only the earthly elements are received in the sacrament as symbols of redemption, the communion with Christ being only by faith. The presence of Christ in the

Lord's Supper, according to Reformed theology, is a presence for faith; and the communion with the body and blood of Christ is a communion by faith. It is not a communion by eating and drinking.

The Lutheran doctrine of real presence was developed in a double antagonism: on the one side to the Roman Catholic doctrine of transubstantiation and the sacrifice of the mass; on the other side to the spiritualizing doctrines of Zwingli and Calvin, which, with all their difference, agree in denying the presence of the body and blood in the elements. The controversy of Lutheranism with Reformed theology is partly exegetical, revolving on the meaning of the words, "This is my body," partly dogmatic, regarding the possibility of Christ being present with His body. Lutheran theology maintains this possibility on the ground of the communication of the divine majesty to the human nature of Christ.

To preclude all explaining of the real presence away Lutheran theology uses expressions like "true, real, substantial body" and "oral manducation." The latter expression means eating with the mouth, and is set in contrast with a figurative eating by faith. But Lutheranism abhors all gross, Capernaitic views. In the controversies of the sixteenth century the prepositions "in, with and under" were made a Lutheran shibboleth.

SACRAMENTS

Baptism and the Lord's Supper are called sacraments. The term, which is not biblical, represents a general conception, embracing those ordinances of Christ through which the grace of salvation is individually conferred, and in which the Word of God is connected with divinely appointed visible elements.

The number of rites called sacraments wavered for a long time in the Church. Finally in the twelfth century the number became fixed at seven: baptism, the mass, confession, ordination, marriage, confirmation and extreme unction. These are still accepted in the Roman Catholic Church. In the Reformation the number of sacraments was fixed at two: baptism and the Lord's Supper. But at first there was some wavering, as can be seen in the Augsburg Confession and the Apology. In accordance with the definition of a sacrament as a divine institution with a promise of grace attached, absolution and in a qualified sense ordination were recognized as sacraments; but they were excluded when the usage became established to include also the external element as an essential part of a sacrament.

To make a sacrament complete in form three things are necessary: the recitation of the words of institution, the giving of the sacrament, and its reception.

ELECTION CONSUMMATED

When the grace of the Holy Spirit has been applied in the means of grace until the end of a human life, then the gracious will of God that provides redemption is disclosed to be a special will, which saves the sinner finally and unalterably, or which has affected the sinner in vain and has failed of realization.

Before proceeding to the elucidation of this paragraph two cautions must be given to the student. First, the preconception popularly expressed in the phrase, "It was to be," is erroneous. That preconception does not fit a living world, a world in the making. It arises from a false method of reasoning. The end is looked at first; the result is assumed to be inevitable, which it is not; every step in the process is also assumed to be inevitable, which is a denial of all contingencies; the process is really not a process in which results are worked out, but a mechanical necessity in which every part inevitably falls into its place. That is not a Christian view of the world. In life and in history and even in natural order it is simply not true that whatever is was to be, that all is simply the expression of an absolute will. In the religious history of mankind and in the religious life of man, according to scriptural principles, the salvation of men is the real outcome of living in relation to God's provision of grace in Christ. The whole thing is not decided before the offer of salvation is made.

Secondly, the Scripture word "election" should be studied by the student with the help of New Testament lexicons and critical commentaries. Brief reference has been made to this word in the section treating of The Gracious Will of God, Chap. V. The chief point is that the word expresses God's personal love to an individual, and it does not denote a selection of certain persons for salvation with the implied rejection of the rest. What Davidson in his Old Testament Theology, p. 132, says with reference to the figure of the potter in Jeremiah, ch. 18, is applicable to the whole teaching of Scripture. He says: "It is meant to show that God deals with men and nations on moral principles, one way or another, according to their character."

Now we will proceed with the elucidation of the paragraph at the head. The eternal purpose of God to save the world through Christ was discussed in Chapter V. There the gracious will of God was considered in its universal relations. It is necessary to look at this gracious will of God once more in its particular relation to an individual life that is completed on earth. We have to do here with what the old dogmaticians called the consequent will of God, in contrast with the antecedent will.

The result of the work of redemption at the close of a life on earth is before us. That result may be final salvation or its contrary. Here these fundamental truths must be kept in mind. All salvation is by grace, all failure to attain salvation is by sin. The grace is entirely from God, the sin entirely from man. If therefore a man is finally saved, that result must be ascribed to the love of God in Christ, in other words, to His gracious will, purpose, election, predestination and foreknowing. If he is not saved finally, it is not due to a want of God's love, will and election, but it is in contravention of these and is to be ascribed solely to man's evil will. The election of God is realized historically and it is not concluded and sealed up for any man until his life on earth is done.

The election of God dare not be divorced from the plan of redemption, and that plan, which has so far been unfolded in its main features in this book, brings out clearly the following features of God's gracious will in Christ in relation to the individual life.

First, God's saving will is not absolute with regard to any individual. The will of God works from above into the world for the realization of salvation, but it also works through the world and in the sphere of finite wills, which are influenced but not coerced by grace. The result is not fixed beforehand, but is the real result of the operation of the divine will of love upon the human will.

Secondly, God's will of grace is not irresistible. Jesus was not picturing an unreality when He said: "How often would I have gathered thy children together, and ye would not." Mt 23:37.

Thirdly, God's will of grace is self-limited. It is limited by an order of salvation ordained by Himself. The will is formed in Christ, applied by the Spirit, and effectual through the means of grace. Nor is there a hidden will at work outside of this order of salvation to determine the result.

The will of God is conditioned in its operation by those conditions which it has itself laid down and embraced in the purpose of redemption in Christ. Men are saved by faith in Christ. That is God's will, purpose, predestination and election. Where the condition is not fulfilled, the election of grace does not stand. "By their unbelief they were broken off, and thou standest by thy faith," Ro 11:20. In view of this truth the theologians of the seventeenth century said that election was from foreseen faith or in view of faith. This form of expression may perhaps be justly criticized, but the thought is correct. Election is not on account of faith, but it is by an order of salvation which is only realized by faith. The question why one man believes and another does not or falls from faith, is another question, and it is not solved by election. After all is said that can be said, there will remain an insoluble element in it. Scripture limits itself to teach that faith is God's gift and unbelief the work of sin.

Scholastic Lutheran theology limited election to the "*finaliter credentes*," those who believe at death. This gives point to an important truth. The finally elect are the finally believing. But in the New Testament the word elect is not so rigidly applied. There, believers are the called and the elect. As it is possible to fall from faith, it is also possible to fall from the calling of God and from the election, as the word is used sometimes in the New Testament, as for instance 1 Th 1:4 (with which compare 5:9, 23) and 2 Pet. 1:10. The latter is not a meaningless admonition: "Make your calling and election sure."

CHAPTER X
REDEMPTION CONSUMMATED

THE COMMUNION OF MAN WITH GOD CONSUMMATED IN THE WORLD TO COME

THE LAST THINGS

The eternal purpose of God, which in its initial stage was realized in creation, which then was disturbed by sin, and which was again restored in the redemption of Christ in the form of saving grace, is steadily advancing through the successive stages of the world toward complete realization. This consummation of God's plan must be considered from three points of view, according to its relation to the individual, to the Church, and to the world.

The term "Last Things," from which is formed the technical term Eschatology, is a term convenient for its comprehensiveness, but very indefinite. It is used to embrace the doctrines connected with the end of human life, of human history, and of the world. This last part of dogmatics treats not merely of things that come last temporally, but of the goal, the fulfillment of all that was designed by God from the beginning, the completion of redemption and the perfection of the kingdom of God.

The individual end comes in death. Then there arises the inquiry about the state after death. For the Church there shall be a finality of development at the coming again of Christ. Many important matters are connected with this event, such as the evangelization of the world, the destiny of

Israel, the Antichrist, the millennium, the resurrection and the final judgment. For the world there is predicted an end and then a new aeon of eternal life.

In regard to all these matters, hidden in the womb of the future or in the mystery of the world beyond, it is becoming to speak with modesty and not with too great assurance. From experience we can have no knowledge of these things; for our judgments we are wholly dependent upon the interpretation of statements, allusions, and figurative and symbolic picturings scattered through the Bible. The actual unfolding of the future may be different from what we imagine it will be. The New Testament shows that it was so with devout minds in Israel when Christ came and with the minds of the first Christians, who expected the return of the Lord in their lifetime.

DEATH AND THE STATE AFTER

The dissolution of the union of body and soul in death does not disrupt the communion of the believer with God, nor is it an annihilation either of believers or unbelievers. The state of the soul after death is one of personal consciousness, in blessed fellowship with Christ on the part of believers, and in tormenting separation from God on the part of the ungodly.

Before entering upon details here it is necessary first to make sure of the broad main lines of biblical Christian conception. It is not a true reading of the Bible which leads one to refer everything that is there said of the future glory of the redeemed to souls immediately after death. The great object of Christian hope, according to both Old and New Testament, is not simply to go to heaven when one dies (that is only a part), but it is the coming of the Lord, the day of the Lord and what it shall bring, namely resurrection, judgment, final redemption and perfection. That is to say, it is not only a hope of a life beyond, but a hope of a future of the kingdom of God. From the New Testament it plainly appears that the first disciples expected this return of the Lord very soon. But when the Lord delayed His coming and many passed into death without the sight of His appearing, the question concerning the condition meanwhile of those who fell asleep in Christ became vitally important. Then another element of the Christian hope was brought into more vivid consciousness. Without giving up in the least the great hope in the second coming of Christ and the expectation of perfected redemption on "that day," they realized also that when they departed this life in death they should be with the Lord, that is, in heaven, and that there they should await the glorious manifestation of the children of God at His return to the earth. This part of the Christian hope is dwelt on especially in three places in the New Testament besides the whole book of Revelation, which deals largely with the blessedness of those who had been slain for the Word of God or who otherwise had died in the faith. The three passages are 2 Co 5:1-9; Phil 1:23; and Jn 14:2-3. We will now look briefly at details in regard to death and the state after it.

In theology different forms of death are distinguished: physical, spiritual and eternal death. This is not in disharmony with biblical ideas, but the Bible does not divide up death. In its use there is one death, the whole fact embracing the end of life and all connected with it before and after. This usage prevails where it is sometimes thought only spiritual death is spoken of. When the apostle, as in Eph 2 :1 and Col 2 :13, speaks of being dead through trespasses, he is not using a figure of speech to describe an unsusceptibility to the good, but he means that by trepasses men are under sentence of death, they are in condemnation. So also in Ro 8:6, cf. v. 13. Possibly the word "dead" is used figuratively in Lu 15:24; 1 Tim 5:6; Rev 3:1, although even here the idea is probably not unsusceptible to the good, but in condemnation. The phrase "second death," used in Revelation, denotes the permanent consequences of death for those who have not passed from death to life in Christ. It is what is commonly understood by eternal death. Death is a judgment for sin, Gen 2:17; Ro 6:23. But for the redeemed the sting of death has been extracted, 1 Co 15:54-57.

The Scriptures represent the physical side of death as a separation of soul and body, 2 Co 5:1; 2 Pet 1:14. The soul continues to exist after the separation. Even the Old Testament conception of Sheol with its shadowy half-life includes the continuance of the soul. Accordingly the phrase "gathered unto the fathers" is so significant. It refers not to burial but to what is beyond the grave. The body, notwithstanding its dissolution, is not altogether annihilated. The truth of resurrection requires that in some sense it also is preserved.

Between death and the resurrection, then, the soul is in an intermediate state. The Old Testament conception of this was imperfect, but the whole of it was not wrapped up in the idea of Sheol. There was other light. All the dead went to Sheol, an underworld of darkness and shadowy flickering existence. Those in it are not spoken of as souls, but as "rephaim," which means the flabby, flaccid. Nevertheless in their silent, drowsy existence they are not unconscious, as the poetical descriptions in Job 3:13-19; Is 14:9-11; Ez 32:21 show. Old Testament believers looked with horror towards

Sheol. But in their faith they overleaped the dread thought of it and with confidence in the God of the living they believed that even death could not separate them from their fellowship with God. Cf. Ps. 49:15; 73:24; Job 19:25-27. They looked for the day of the Lord, which should bring their final redemption, and in later Old Testament times saw the gloom of Sheol dispelled in the hope of resurrection.

In the New Testament disembodied souls are called spirits, Heb 12:23; 1 Pet 3:19, and souls, Rev 6:9, etc. They are conscious. As constituting a people of God, a multitude, as belonging to the city of God, the heavenly Jerusalem, worshipping God, the redeemed are in active fellowship with one another, Rev 7:9; 19:6, etc.; Heb. 12:22; Gal 4:26. And they are in fellowship with Christ, Lu 23:43; 2 Co 5:8 ; Phil 1:23. The idea of many modern theologians that they are clothed with some kind of ethereal body cannot be summarily dismissed as fanciful. St. Paul in 1 Co 5:1 seems to allude to something of this kind. However, we prefer to think that by the house not made with hands the apostle means not a bodily, but a personal form of being. The lost souls, being in torment, are conscious, Lu 16:23. The fact that the disembodied souls are consciously active contradicts the theory of the sleep of the soul or psychopannychism. This notion, held by many in different ages and now taught by Adventists, has been even charged to Luther. But Luther did not advocate the idea of soul-sleep; he taught that "the dead are outside of all time," that "we depart and come again on the last day sooner than we shall be aware of it, and will not know how long we have been away." Death is frequently called sleep in the Bible, but this is an expression for rest from the labors of life. Cf. Rev 14:13; Is 57:2; and the description in Job 3 :13.

The intermediate state is not one of development in moral and spiritual progress. Death fixes the spiritual state of man, and after it the soul experiences no growth in grace or in sin. This implies that death itself effects a release from all the power of sin in the saved. No conjectures suggested by sympathy for the lost or by perplexity over the salvation of the heathen can shake the clear teaching of the Bible that death fixes the future state. The theory of aprobation after death is attractive as a means to solve unresolved problems, but it is in conflict with the uniform teaching of Scripture. After death there is no possibility of falling from grace and no possibility of conversion. Passages like 2 Co 5:10; 6:2; Heb 3:7; 9:27; Lu 16:29 are too explicit. When the idea of a future probation is extracted from 1 Pet 3:19; 4:6; Phil 2:10, it is by misinterpretation. The first of these passages teaches not a preaching of salvation, but of condemnation; the second speaks of an evangelizing of the dead not in death, but while they lived on earth ; the third does not say that every knee shall bow in faith. We subscribe to the cautious words of Thomasius :

> The sharp contrast between faith and unbelief, between the sons of God and those of disobedience, which runs through all Scripture, forbids this view. Of him who persists in unbelief it is said: The wrath of God abideth on him, Jn 3:36. If they reject the testimony of Christ, it shall be a testimony against them in the day of judgment, Mt 10:18; Jn 12:48."

In the intermediate state, souls are in a provisional condition of blessedness or misery, waiting for the full realization of their final state at the resurrection on the last day. The theory of conditional immortality, that is, of the annihilation of the ungodly after aprobation after death, is simply an effort to escape from the dreadful truth of eternal punishment, which is explicitly taught by Christ and the apostles.

Departed souls are beyond the conditions of space and time which belong to life on earth; but they are in such locality as spirits are capable of. The Scriptures name various abiding places of the dead. The Old Testament name for the place of the dead is Sheol, conceived as a region under the earth, in which all the dead, good and wicked, are kept in a dark, feeble existence with wavering memory and knowledge. This conception of Sheol shows how undeveloped were the ideas of the state after death in the Old Testament. In later Jewish belief there was an advance so that the pious and the wicked were separated in Sheol. This is the conception which underlies the Lord's parable in Lu 16:19. In the New Testament Hades represents the Sheol of the Old Testament. Gehenna is the name taken over from Jewish speech for that part of Hades where the wicked suffer punishment, which punishment is by fire. Cf. Mt 5:22; 18:9, etc. Synonymous with Hades sometimes the word abyss is used, as in Ro 10:7, but sometimes abyss is equivalent to Gehenna, as in Rev 20:1. Paradise in Lu 23:43 and Abraham's bosom in Lu 16:19 appear to be equivalent expressions for the part of Hades where the righteous are. That departed saints are in Heaven is an inference from the fact that they are with Christ, who is in heaven, Jn 14 :3 ; 2 Co 5 :8 ; Phil 1 :23.

Scholastic theology in the Middle Ages developed the conception, which still holds in the Roman Catholic Church, that there are five receptacles for the dead : hell, the place of the damned; purgatory, the place for the completion of penance by the saved; *limbus puerorum*, where unbaptized infants suffer the loss but not the pain of damnation; *limbus patrum*, the abode of the Old Testament saints, now vacant since Christ by His descent into Hades has led them into paradise; and heaven, the permanent abode of all the redeemed. Protestantism rejected this scheme and retained only two places, heaven and hell. It objects most strongly to the doctrine of purgatory as a superstition which conflicts with the sufficiency of the redemption of Christ to cleanse from all sin. It objects to the conception of a *limbus* in hell for unbaptized infants as resting upon the absolute necessity of baptism for salvation.

In utterly discarding the idea of the Old Testament saints having been kept in the underworld until released by Christ, the old Protestants went farther than many modern Bible students are willing to go. The question is whether the Old Testament representations of Sheol merely represent imperfect popular conceptions or whether they stand for the actually existing fact in that preparatory period? If the latter view is correct, there is undoubtedly some foundation for the belief, which is very ancient, that the descent of Christ into Hades effected a blissful change in the state of the righteous there, raising them to the privileges of those who have since departed in Christ. We are not able to find any direct scriptural testimony for this idea. It must be left to the field of conjecture.

EVENTS PRECEDING THE SECOND COMING OF CHRIST

The consummation of the work of redemption shall be preceded by a series of events, known by scriptural predictions, which shall bring the Church to the end of its development and prepare the world for the coming again of Christ. These events are the evangelization of the world, the conversion of Israel, and the final trial of the Church in the manifestation of Antichrist.

The universal character of Christianity implies universal evangelization. The fact is partly implied, partly directly predicted in Old Testament prophecy. It is implied in the promise given to Abraham, Gen 12:3 ; it is expressed especially in the glowing portrayals of Isaiah, Is 2:2.; 56:7, etc. This evangelization before the end was distinctly foretold by Christ, Mt 24:14; Mk 13:10; Mt 28:19; Lu 24:47. The goal is indicated in St. Paul's phrase "the fullness of the Gentiles," Ro 11:25. This expression means universal evangelization, not necessarily universal conversion. With it shall come the salvation of "all Israel."

The conversion of Israel is included in the prophetic promises in the Old Testament of a restoration of the chosen people. It is a violent exegesis which would transfer these promises, the constant theme of the prophets, to a spiritual Israel. Nor can the distinct prediction of the conversion of Israel by St. Paul, in Ro 11:11-29, be turned from God's ancient people to a spiritual Israel, that is, Christians generally. The words "all Israel shall be saved" do not necessarily mean that numerically all Jews shall be converted, but enough of them to represent the race. This indubitable prophecy has been materialized by some imaginative people, who press the letter of prophetic language, into an earthly exaltation of the Jewish nation, according to which the Jews shall return to the Holy Land, Jerusalem shall become the spiritual capital of the world, the temple shall be rebuilt and its ritual services restored. All this is part of a chiliastic scheme, which a sober interpretation of the Scriptures must reject. It may be remarked here (and the remark will also bear on matters which follow) that the biblical prophets necessarily found the dress for their predictions in the existing historical conditions of their day. In the fulfillment the historical circumstances are different. Therefore it is necessary to distinguish between the historical dress and the doctrinal principle of prophecy.

Whatever may be the prosperity and extension, which the Church shall yet enjoy before the end comes, it shall pass through fearful trials. The persecutions of the Church at its beginning are a prototype of this. This final great trial is predicted in the great eschatological discourse of Christ, Mt 24:10-13 and parallels. It was also foretold in various places by St. Paul, e. g., 1 Tim 4:1; 2 Tim 3:1. It was referred to by St. Peter 2 Pet 3:3-4. Then there shall be a great apostasy, 2 Th 2:3; severe tribulation for the Church, Mt 24:21; the appearance of false prophets, Mt 24:11, 24; and the manifestation of Antichrist.

What is the Antichrist? The concentration of all the powers hostile to Christ either in a polity or a person, probably the latter. The revelation of Christ in the history of the world and in the extension of the Church is also forcing the evil in the world to a consummation and to a full and final manifestation of itself before it shall be ultimately overcome through the parousia, the appearance of Christ. The name Antichrist is found only in the first epistle of St. John, who uses it in the plural as well as in the singular, 1 Jn 2:18 ; 4 :3. In the great eschatological discourse the Lord predicted the coming of false Christs, Mt 24:24. St Paul depicts the man of sin in 2 Th 2:3-10, the most specific passage on the Antichrist in the New Testament. The teaching of the New Testament on this subject is a development of ideas everywhere pervading Old Testament prophecy, which represents the kingdom of God in conflict with the hostile powers of the world and its final establishment through the overthrow of those powers. Ezekiel sees the last attack upon the chosen people of God as a gathering of hostile nations in the land of Magog under a king called Gog. Cf. Ez chapters 38 and 39. Daniel sees the same conflict in the arising of various beasts and horns among the nations of the world, reaching a climax in an especially arrogant and wicked king, who shall profane the sanctuary and set up the abomination that maketh desolate. Cf. especially Dan ch. 11. The correspondence of this king with the arch-enemy of the Jews and their religion in the times of the Maccabees, Antiochus Epiphanes, is unmistakable. But his furious effort does not exhaust the contents of the prophecy. In a manner similar to Daniel the book of Revelation describes the arising of various kinds of beasts hostile to the Church. Going behind the outward form to the essential idea running through these representations, we observe that Antichrist is the principle of hostility to God and Christ in the supreme display of its Satanic power and malignity. The clearest description of this evil principle is that of St. Paul in 2 Th 2:3-10, which appears to be set upon the background of Danielic predictions. This principle of "lawlessness" is at work in all ages. St. Paul saw it at the beginning of the Church in Jewish hostility, 2 Th 2:7; and St. John at a later day in the deniers of Christ's humanity, who had invaded the Church. It is therefore not surprising that in every period of the Church pious minds have recognized Antichrist in any specially oppressive form of hostility to Christ or of wickedness existing at the time. The Reformers and Lutheran theologians after them identified the papacy with Antichrist. The principle of Antichrist shall be "revealed in his own season" before Christ comes, that is, fully and finally manifested, and this manifestation shall be personal as "the man of sin, the lawless one," who is doomed to perdition. The Antichrist of the last times shall be not only an iniquitous system or polity within or without the Church, but a person in whom the power of evil in the world shall be concentrated.

THE PAROUSIA

The second advent of Christ shall bring the completion of the work of redemption. It shall be accompanied by the general resurrection and the judgment. The idea that it shall be preceded by a millennium and the idea that it shall be the introduction of a millennium before the final consummation of the kingdom of God are both to be rejected.

The second coming of Christ at the end of time is as much a part of the Christian system of truth as the incarnation. In the first age of the Church this event was eagerly anticipated, and in all periods it has formed a part of the faith confessed by the Church, as in the Apostles' Creed. The work of redemption, which embraces not only the preparation of men for death, but also their glorification, and furthermore not only the glorification of the elect, but also of the world—this universal redemption still awaits its consummation. Herein lies the significance of Christ's return. The great goal of Christian hope according to the New Testament is the second advent of Christ in glory. No theme is perhaps more frequently mentioned in the New Testament than the parousia, the presence, the epiphaneia, the appearing, or the day of the Son of man. Our Lord made this a prominent part of His teaching, especially in the great eschatological discourse, Mt ch. 24. Cf. also Lu 12:35.40; 17:22-37. The apostolic writings are full of references to it, and many of them are of such a character that it is evident from them that the apostolic Church regarded the day as near at hand.

The appearing of the Lord from heaven shall be a visible appearance of the incarnate One, Act 1:11; Mt 16:27-28; Rev 1:7. It shall be sudden, Lu 21:34; 1 Th 5:3; 2 Pet 3:10; in a definite moment of time, which in spite of the symbolic numbers in Daniel and Revelation and the calculations based on them, is incalculable, Mk 13:32; Act 1:7. Some chiliasts imagine a twofold coming of Christ, one at the beginning and another at the end of the millennium. But this view must be rejected with the whole millennial doctrine.

That the second coming of Christ is connected with what is said about a millennium in Rev 20:1-10, is undeniable. But what is really said, that is, meant there, is doubtful. That is the pivot of all millennial theories, and it is a very insecure basis for a millennial doctrine. It must be emphasized that this is the only place in the Bible where the term millennium occurs. In approaching this subject it behooves a Lutheran to be free from bias, a bias to which he may be exposed because chiliasm is rejected in the Augsburg Confession. Notwithstanding this confessional utterance many Lutherans, just like many Christians in other communions, have embraced millennialism in some one of its manifold forms.

The fundamental feature of millennialism is that there shall be a long time of religious glory on earth, introduced by the visible or invisible appearing of Christ, as a transition to the everlasting glory. It is customary to distinguish three types, which used to be characterized as gross, more subtle, and most subtle chiliasm, and which we may designate sensuous, refined, and spiritualizing millennialism. Sensuous chiliasm expects a worldly kingdom of the saints on earth with sensuous enjoyments. Such were the "Jewish opinions" condemned by the Augsburg Confession, Article XVII. Refined chiliasm (known as Premillennialism) reads the final history of the Church in an order like this: The Lord appears visibly, destroys Antichrist and his kingdom, binds Satan, and gathers believing Israel; the elite of the saints or all the saints rise from the dead (the first resurrection), the Lord and His saints reign over the world from Jerusalem for 1,000 years (1,000 being a round number) and extraordinary missionary activity prevails; then Satan is loosed for a time, seduces believers, collects the nations (Gog and Magog) for a final conflict with the Lord and His kingdom, is defeated by fire from heaven and cast into the lake of fire. Spiritualizing chiliasm (known as Postmillennialism) regards the coming of Christ as invisible and His reign as a spiritual rule from heaven, which effects an extraordinary development and prosperity of the Church, as a preliminary perfection of it before the powers of wickedness break loose for the final conflict and the end comes.

What foundation has millennialism in any of its forms in Scripture? Before stating the facts, which shall be done only briefly, it should be remarked that millennial belief is older than the Christian Church. We lay no stress on the fact that it is found in Zoroastrianism; but it is significant that the belief had spread among the Jews before Christ, for it is possible that it passed to the Christian Church from that source. There is no millennialism in the Old Testament. The prophets only picture a blessed reign of God on earth in Messianic times. It has been truly said: "Christ, the Lord, was no chiliast." He predicts only His coming to judgment at the end of the world. Nor do the epistles go beyond this idea. Millennialists read the belief into the epistles as into all Scripture; but to insert a millennium into a forced crevice in 1 Th 4:13-18 or 1 Co 15:22-28 is arbitrary. There remains only Rev 20:4-7, which does speak of a millennium. But let it be remembered it is a millennium in a vision, a vision expressed in symbols. Such visions must not be read as a narrative of future history; they must be resolved (if that is possible) to the principles which they exhibit in symbolism. The book of Revelation is confessedly difficult and doubtful in its interpretation. They who speak dogmatically of its meaning are rash. Therefore without attempting an interpretation of Rev 20, we follow the clear teaching found in the utterances of Christ and of the epistles, which leave no room for a millennium. If an interpretation of the thousand years in Rev 20 should be insisted on, we should prefer to regard it as the symbolic number for the highest perfection (ten raised to the third power). It would then be descriptive of the perfected kingdom of Christ. But if the thousand years must be understood of a period in the history of the Church, we freely acknowledge that the chiliastic interpretation is to be preferred to that unnatural interpretation, which was introduced by Augustine and continued down to the orthodox theology of the seventeenth century and beyond, and which conceives it as a historical period in the past, beginning with the Christian era, or the age of Constantine, or that of Charles the Great.

The second advent of Christ shall be attended by the general resurrection, 1 Co 15:23; 1 Th 4:16; 2 Th 2:1, etc. Resurrection embraces both the restoration of the bodies which were dissolved in death and their reunion with their proper souls. Those alive at the parousia of Christ shall experience a transformation without resurrection, 1 Co 15:51. The dissolution of the body in death is not without redemptive significance, for, as Luther suggests in the Large Catechism, it is a purgation from inherent sin. The doctrine of resurrection is found only in the later books of the Old Testament. The idea is applied to the people of Israel in the prophets, Is 26:19; Ez 37:5; afterwards to individual resurrection, Job 19:25; Dan 12:2. In the time between the two Testaments and at the beginning of the Christian era it was ardently believed by devout Jews, notably the Pharisees, but denied by the Sadducees. It is abundantly taught in the New Testament, although chiefly with reference to believers. But that there is also to be a resurrection of the unbelieving and wicked appears from various statements, Jn 5:28, 29; Act 24:15; Rev 20:13. It is implied in the judgment scene in Mt 25:31. The belief in a double resurrection, separated by an interval of time, falls with the millennial doctrine. The "first resurrection," mentioned in Rev 20:6, is not temporally, but qualitatively distinct from the resurrection of the others. The phrase is used in contrast with "second death," used in the same connection and in ch. 2:11, and explained in Rev 20:14 and 21:8. The first resurrection means that those who participate in the resurrection to life are at the end of all judgment, whereas the others shall rise only to receive final condemnation and eternal death. In short, the first resurrection is the same as the resurrection of the just, Lu 14:14; Act 24:15. It is what St. Paul calls the resurrection in Phil 3:11. The resurrection of both just and unjust shall be on the last day. We can form no adequate conception of the bodies that rise. Those of the redeemed are described as glorified, spiritual bodies, which, whatever else it means, certainly implies a perfect organ for the spirit within, Dan

12:3; Mt 13:43; Phil 3:21; 1 Co 15:40. The bodies of those who become the prey of second death shall doubtless correspond to their moral condition. Questions as to difference of sexes and the results of changes produced by age in this life in connection with the resurrection are curious rather than important. The old idea of eternal youth is as good as any other. The identity of the future body with the present body must be maintained, however this identity may be imagined, whether as a restoration of the same material particles, which, however, appears to be against the analogy in 1 Co 15:37, or as a persisting form underlying the changing matter of the body. The Scriptures teach resurrection, not the creation of an organism altogether new.

The general resurrection shall be followed by the final judgment. Both good and evil in this world are developing to ripeness. In the end there shall be a separation. This shall come by a judgment pronounced by Christ, Jn 5:22, 27; Act 10:42. A correct view of the judgment cannot be obtained unless it is connected with redemption, Lu 21:28. For the redeemed it is the completion of their redemption. The judgment is a sifting and a separation, as is vividly portrayed in the Lord's picture in Mt 25:31. The glorious liberty of the children of God can only be manifested by the removal of the elements hostile to the kingdom of God, Ro 8:19-21. As to the time of the judgment nothing further can be said than that it is the last day, Jn 12:48. As to the place no inference can be made. The figure of the lightning in Lu 17:24, which lightens from one part under heaven unto the other part, suggests that it may be everywhere upon the earth. The valley of Jehosaphat, mentioned in the prophecy of Joel, 3:2, cannot be taken literally. That all men shall be judged is explicitly stated, 2 Co 5:10; Act 10:42; 17:31. Our Lord's word, that he

that heareth His word and believeth, cometh not into
judgment, Jn 5:24, is not contradictory to this statement. The
believer shall pass through the judgment unscathed and not
come into condemnation, 1 Jn 4:17. The description in Mt
25:31 also shows that the judgment shall not be an
investigation into life and conduct to discover guilt and
innocence, but a manifestation of what has been worked out
in every life. The standard of judgment shall be the Word of
God, Jn 12:48; Ro 2:16. That Word will determine what has
been the attitude towards Christ and His salvation, Mt 7:21;
10:40-42. The decision is based on works as the evidence of
the attitude of the heart, Mt 16:27; 2 Co 5:10. There is no
conflict in this with the doctrine of salvation by faith, for the
works will prove the faith or unbelief. Even the heathen shall
be judged by their works, Ro 2:6-11. The award shall be
blessedness or its opposite. But different measures of glory to
the redeemed according to different degrees of faithfulness
are probable, 1 Co 15:41; Mt 10:41; 19:28; Lu 19:17; 22:30.
This thought is countenanced in the Apology of the
Augsburg Confession. But all such honors are rewards of
grace.

THE END OF THE WORLD

*Sin disturbs not only the life of man, but also the order of the world,
which is not only physical, but also moral. Redemption therefore shall
bring vast changes into the world. The transition from the present order
to the new order of glory is called the end of the world. It shall follow the
parousia of Christ and the judgment.*

"A new heaven and a new earth, wherein dwelleth
righteousness." This is the object of hope in connection with

the manifestation of redemption, which is set forth in Old Testament prophecy, Is 65:17; 66:22, and repeated in the New Testament, 2 Pet 3:13; Rev 21:1; Ro 8:21. The world in its present form shall come to an end. The old Lutheran theologians conceived of this as an annihilation of the universe. But what the Bible teaches is "the regeneration," Mt 19:28, the "restoration of all things," Acts 3:21. The lurid language of "fire" in various places in the Scriptures, especially in 2 Pet 3:7, is expressive of the thoroughness of the judgment which shall come upon "ungodly men." The end shall consist in a change of the quality of the world, not in an annihilation of the substance of the universe; as Luther beautifully put it: "The heavens now have on their workday clothes, but then they shall put on their Sunday dress." However, the new order shall be introduced with mighty convulsions in nature, Heb 12:26, 27; 2 Pet 3:7-13; Mt 24:29. The goal in the great transformation is a suitable "tabernacle of God with men," Rev 21:9.

ETERNAL LIFE AND DEATH

The new heaven and the new earth shall be the scene of the final realization of God's purpose of creation and redemption. Those who have excluded themselves from the fellowship of God and whose exclusion has become fixed in the final judgment shall exist in separation from the righteous in eternal misery. The redeemed shall have the eternal fruition of God's presence in blessedness and glory. This is the distinction between eternal death and eternal life.

Eternal life is potentially the possession of believers here. In full realization it is the inheritance of the saints in the world to come. The essence of eternal life is, as Christians in all ages have conceived, the vision and fruition of God, 1 Jn 3:2; 1 Co 13:12; Rev 22:4. It is the state of perfect bliss, which is described in a great variety of ways, more or less figurative, in the Bible.

The essence of eternal condemnation is exclusion from communion with God and Christ. It is the second death. It is a state of misery, variously described in pictorial language in the New Testament as destruction, outer darkness, hell fire, etc. That the state of condemnation is eternal should not be doubted in view of the very explicit and strong statements of Christ and the apostles, Mt 25:41, 46; Mk 9:44; 2 Th 1:9, etc. There is therefore no scriptural basis for theories which try to explain away the dread fact, like the theory of the annihilation of the wicked or that of universal restoration. Harrowing as is the thought of the eternal condemnation of the lost to our minds, the believer in the Scriptures must accept it as the truth which Christ Himself made Himself responsible for.

The kingdom of Christ shall be perfected in the world of glory that is to come. Then the rule of God shall be perfectly realized. Then, according to the testimony of the apostle Paul, Christ, having completed His work of redemption, shall deliver up the kingdom to God, 1 Co 15:24, and God shall be all in all, 1 Co 15:28. The perfected redemption of Christ shall make eternally manifest that the end of the ways of God, the goal of the history of the world, is the glory of God in the fellowship of the saints. "For of Him, and through Him, and unto Him are all things," Ro 11:36.

6605508R00133

Made in the USA
San Bernardino, CA
11 December 2013